Contents

Foreword

This book has very simple purposes: to describe the general structural design of English and to focus against it those special difficulties commonly encountered when we are learning to write the language. Intended primarily for teachers and students of English Composition, it may serve other readers—particularly those interested in literary exegesis —as a succinct, elementary, linguistic introduction to English syntax. I should hasten to add, however, that the book was not written with my fellow linguists in mind, that certain distributional methods fruitful in technical linguistics are not used here, and that pedagogical simplicity rather than linguistic consistency determined the inductive approach to the subject matter.

Modern structural linguistics has been compared in method with field physics, quantum mechanics, discrete mathematics, and Gestalt psychology. Its success in discovering fundamental descriptive units that can be isolated by rigid analytical procedures has made it the envy of the other social sciences if, sometimes, the despair of the humanities. One must admit that linguistics involves a somewhat specialized manner of thinking about the process and system of language, and that its terminology and working symbolism are little known at present either to the general public or to the public for whom this book is particularly intended. Preoccupied with the theory of their subject, or with the structural description of *spoken* languages, or with the oral-aural teaching of *spoken* languages, the linguists themselves have, for the most part, shown little interest in the application of their methods and results to that most important area of language pedagogy— the course in English composition. Yet it is exactly here that precision and simplicity of linguistic description are most urgently needed, most immediately and widely useful. The task of educational adaptation, however, is not an easy one. A bridge of explanation between the old and the new, between the traditional and linguistic approaches to composition teaching, must be erected very cautiously and carefully. This book, although not constituting such a bridge in its entirety, is intended to provide some essential caissons, piers, and arches.

I am greatly indebted to many predecessors, and particularly to Sweet, Jespersen, Trnka, Kruisinga, de Groot, and Hjelmslev. I owe an obvious and very special debt to Bloomfield, Fries, Nida, Trager and Smith, Pike, Lotz, Jakobson, Harris, Twaddell, Hill, and my colleagues of the Indiana University Linguistics Seminar. As far as possible, however, I have tried to re-examine each problem from my own standpoint and in my own experiential terms, and I have not hesitated to modify, curtail, expand, revamp, or replace the prior explanations of others whenever my thinking or the demands of pedagogical expediency suggested change. There is danger here, of course—danger that the blend of old and new, linguistic terminology with traditional part-of-speech labels, synchronism with a dash of diachronism, of a treatment sometimes too obvious, sometimes too involved, sometimes too compressed, sometimes too diffuse may in the long run please nobody. My experience with two limited preliminary mimeographed editions of the book in the classroom and on television indicates that the result is at least practical.

And now, as Chaucer says (*Hous of Fame* II, 148 ff.):

> Thou goost hoom to the hous anoon,
> And, also domb as any stoon,
> Thou sittest at another boke,
> Til fully daswed is thy loke.

HAROLD WHITEHALL

Bloomington, Indiana

1 Writing and speech

1.1 All of us have a grammar. The fact that we use and understand English in daily affairs means that we use and understand, for the most part unconsciously, the major grammatical patterns of our language. Yet because of the effects of education, many of us have come to think of a relatively formal written English and its reflection among those who "speak by the book" as the only genuine English, and to consider its grammar as the only acceptable English grammar. That is by no means true. The basic form of present-day American English is the patterned, rhythmed, and segmented code of voice signals called *speech*—speech as used in everyday conversation by highly educated people (*cultivated speech*), by the general run of our population (*common speech*), or by some rural persons in such geographically isolated areas as the Ozark Plateau, the Appalachian Mountains, or the woodland areas of northern New England (*folk speech*). From the code of speech, the language of formal writing is something of an abstraction, differing in details of grammar and vocabulary and lacking clear indication of the bodily gestures and meaningful qualities of the voice which accompany ordinary conversation. Thus, serious written English may be regarded as a rather artificial dialect of our language. To acquire that dialect, the would-be writer needs to know a good deal about its structural details, and particularly about those in which it differs from the less formal varieties of speech.

1.2 Even a moment's reflection will show that the spoken American language is backed by expressive features lacking in the written language: the rise or fall of the voice at the ends of phrases and sentences; the application of vocal loudness to this or that word or part of a word; the use of gesture; the meaningful rasp or liquidity, shouting or muting, drawling or clipping, whining or breaking, melody or whispering imparted to the quality of the voice. Written English, lacking clear indication of such features, must be so managed that it compensates for what it lacks. It must be more carefully organized than speech in order to overcome its communicative deficiencies as compared with speech. In speech, we safeguard meaning by the use of intonation, stress, gesture, and voice qualities. In writing, we must deal with our medium in such a way that the meaning cannot possibly be misunderstood. In the absence of an actual hearer capable of interrupting and demanding further explanation, a clear writer is always conscious of "a reader over his shoulder." All this despite the fact that writing, being permanent, as compared with speech, which is evanescent, allows not only reading but also rereading.

1.3 Nor is this all. If written English is somewhat abstract, somewhat artificial, it is also generalized—national, not geographically or socially limited in scope. We must realize that comparatively few of us make use in our day-to-day affairs of a generalized spoken American English that is at all comparable with it. Such a language—a Received Standard Spoken English—exists, but not for the most part in this country where the practical need for it is slight. It exists in England, where the practical need for it is great. In England, many people still start their linguistic careers speaking one or another of the regional dialects, dialects so different from each other in vocabulary and grammar, so quilt-crazy in their distribution, that they form real barriers to generalized, national communication. Yet, in a modern, democratic country, general communication is a necessity. For that reason, Englishmen are willing to accept the notion both of a generalized spoken and a generalized written form of expression on a level above the dialects, and are willing to make the effort of learning them in school and elsewhere. We would be equally willing if our everyday speech happened to resemble this specimen from the English county of Lancaster:

> "Nay! my heart misgi'es me! There's summat abeawt this neet's wark as is noan jannock. Look thee here! Yon chap's noan t' first sheep theaw's lifted tax-free fro't' mooar, an' aw've niver been one to worrit abeawt it, that aw hav'nt. But toneet, someheaw, it's noan t'same. There's summat beawn't 'appen—aw con feel it i' my booans. This een, an unconny wind wor burrin' i't'ling, an' not a cleawd i't' sky; an' whin aw went deawn to' t'well for watter, t'bats wor flyin' reawn it in a widdershins ring. Mark my words, there's mooar to coom."

1.4   In the United States, our language situation is quite different. Ours is probably the only country on earth in which three thousand miles of travel will bring no difficulty of spoken communication. We do have, of course, regional and social differences of language. The speech of Maine does not coincide in all points with that of Texas, nor the speech of Georgia with that of Minnesota. The speech of cultivated people in urban centers is not precisely that of the general mass of our citizens, nor that of rural residents of limited education in geographically secluded areas. Yet, unless we deliberately choose to emphasize disparities for social or other reasons, our regional and social speech differences create no great barriers to the free exchange of opinions and ideas. They consist of flavoring rather than substance.

1.5 Precisely for that reason, pressures for the adoption of a generalized national spoken American English comparable in acceptance and prestige with Received Standard Spoken British have proved largely unavailing. In American life, one may use cultivated or common speech Southern, cultivated or common speech Northeastern, or cultivated or common speech North Middle Western without encountering any great practical disadvantage. Our standards of speech are mainly regional standards, and most of us, in actual fact, speak some kind of a patois in which one or another of the cultivated or common speech regional varieties of American English blends quite happily with elements absorbed from reading and the educational process. We are very fortunate in this—fortunate that American historical and sociological conditions have removed difficulties of spoken communication found in most other parts of the world.

1.6 In a lesser sense, however, our good fortune is something of a misfortune. Because an American can understand other Americans no matter what regional or social class they come from, he is apt to underestimate the necessity for a generalized and abstract written American English. Because he finds no pressing reason for standardizing his speech, he is likely to misunderstand the necessity for standardizing his writing. He would like to write as he speaks. Moreover, the differences between the various regional and social varieties of American speech, being slight, are often of so subtle a nature that he tends to find difficulty in discriminating them. Slight as they are, when transferred to writing they are sufficient to make a reader pause, to induce a momentary feeling of unfamiliarity, to interrupt his consideration of the *matter* of expression by unwittingly calling attention to the *manner* of expression. Outside frankly literary writing (particularly the writing of poetry), such pauses, such unfamiliarities, such interruptions will hinder rather than help the writer's communicative purpose. If writing must be generalized, it must be generalized with a good reason: to speak with a local accent is not disadvantageous; to write serious prose with a local accent definitely is.

1.7 The moral of all this is clear. To gain command of serious written English is to acquire, quite deliberately, an abstract and generalized variety of the language differing by nature and purpose from any social or regional variety whatsoever. It is to sacrifice the local for the general, the spontaneous for the permanent. It is to bring to the study of written American English something of the perspective we normally reserve for the study of foreign languages. It is to master a set of grammatical and vocabulary patterns not because they are "correct" but because experience has proved them efficient in the communicative activity of writing.

1.8 The word "correct" is deliberately introduced here. The clear distinctions between spoken and written language mentioned in the paragraphs above have been all too often masked by the pernicious doctrine of "correctness." Perhaps that is to be expected. Without the flexible medium of language, a human society in human terms would be impossible. Without language, there could be no continuous record of experience, no diversification of labor, no great social institutions—the humanity of man could never have been achieved. But social activities breed social rituals and social judgments. Because language is *the* basic social instrument, it has inevitably acquired social attitudes so

complex and variegated that they have often been al-
lowed to obscure its primary communicative function.
For far too many of us, knowledge of language is confused with knowledge of judgments on language that
are socially acceptable. Education in the English language has become, for the most part, education in linguistic niceties—a poor substitute for that real linguistic
education which ought to show us the major and minor
patterns of our language, the way in which they interlock
in function, the ways in which they can be manipulated
for effective expression. As a result, the instrument of
communication which should be every man's servant has
become most men's master. This need not be so. Our self-
confidence is immediately bolstered, our attitudes towards the study of writing techniques tremendously im-
proved, once we realize that the difficulties of writing
English do not spring from faulty nurture, restricted
intelligence, or beyond-the-tracks environment but from
the necessary change-over from one kind of English to
another—that they are neither unpardonable nor irreme-
diable.

1.9 Such is the milieu of the written English with
which this little book is concerned. No matter
what irrationalities surround the details and the per-
spectives by which English is normally viewed, the fact
that it has so admirably served and is still serving the
needs of many fine writers guarantees that it is neither
an impossible nor an unworthy instrument of human expression. Let us admit that all languages, spoken or
written, are man-made things, that their weaknesses as
well as their strengths are implicit in their human origin.
Let us admit that the world has never known either a
faultless language nor one constructed on what to us
seems a strictly logical system. The proper approach to
written English is first to understand what the medium
is; then to concede its limitations and to use its strengths
to the best possible effect. Every communicative medium

has a set of resistances that the communicator must overcome. Marble is hard; paint relatively unmanageable; music barely descriptive. No small part of any kind of composition is contributed directly by tensions set up between the craftsman's demands on his medium on the one hand and its inherent resistances on the other. To this, the science, craft, and art of expression in written American English is no exception.

2 | Word-groups

2.1 The grammatical description of any language is made scientifically possible by isolating certain recurrent units of expression and examining their distribution in contexts. The largest of these units are sentences, which can be decomposed into smaller constituent units: first *word-groups*,[1] then the affixes and combining forms entering into the formation of words, and finally the significant speech-sounds (*phonemes*) of the language. Normally, we would first isolate the smallest units (the phonemes) and their written representations and then work up gradually to the sentence units. With written English, however, it is advantageous to reverse this procedure and to start by isolating and classifying the word-groups. Because of the nature of the English language, which, on the one hand, uses word-groups as the main sentence constituents, and, on the other, uses certain word-group types as sentences, the word-group has become our main structural unit of expression—the brick with which we build up edifices of discourse.

[1] This rather clumsy term is used in this book to avoid the traditional distinction between phrase and clause (i.e., dependent subject-predicate word-group).

2.2 In written English, a word-group is a cluster of two or more words which functions either independently or in a longer sequence of statement as a grammatical unit. Thus, the word-group *I was foolish* can function as an independent grammatical unit in the sentence *I was foolish*(.), but it functions as the *complement* in the more extended sentence *He said I was foolish*. Similarly, six constituent word-groups are embodied in the first part of my last sentence: *The word-group I was foolish can function as an independent grammatical unit in the sentence I was foolish*. In spoken English, word-groups are marked off either as independent utterances (spoken sentences) or grammatically significant segments of utterances by various combinations of what have been called *configurational features:* (1) rise or fall in voice *loudness;* (2) rise or fall in voice *tone;* (3) *interruption* of the normal transition between one speech-sound and the next. According to the ways in which they are used and constituted, two main types of English word-groups can be distinguished: *headed* (endocentric) and *non-headed* (exocentric).[2]

2.3 Headed groups have this peculiarity: all the grammatical functions open to them as groups can also be exercised by one expression within them. They are, so to speak, expansions of this expression, called the *head* of the group, and it is possible to substitute the head for the group or the group for the head within the same grammatical frame (i.e., in the same context) without causing any formal dislocation of the overall grammatical structure. For instance, in **Fresh fruit is** *good*(.), the headed word-group *fresh fruit* serves as subject; in *I like* **fresh fruit**(.), it serves as complement. If we substitute the head expression *fruit* for *fresh fruit* in

---

[2] Since the appearance of Bloomfield's remarkable book *Language,* the parenthesized expressions have been rather commonly used by linguists, at least in this country.

either case, the grammatical frame *subject, verb, comple-ment* will remain formally undisturbed:

$$\begin{cases} \textit{Fresh fruit} \text{ is good.} \\ \textit{Fruit} \text{ is good.} \end{cases}$$
$$\begin{cases} \text{I like } \textit{fresh fruit.} \\ \text{I like } \textit{fruit.} \end{cases}$$

Similarly:

$$\begin{cases} \textit{All this nice fresh fruit} \text{ is good.} \\ \textit{Fruit} \text{ is good.} \end{cases}$$
$$\begin{cases} \textit{Singing songs} \text{ is fun.} \\ \textit{Singing} \text{ is fun.} \end{cases}$$
$$\begin{cases} \text{I like } \textit{singing songs.} \\ \text{I like } \textit{singing.} \end{cases}$$
$$\begin{cases} \textit{Singing Mary songs} \text{ is fun.} \\ \textit{Singing} \text{ is fun.} \end{cases}$$

In these sets of examples, the head expressions *fruit* and *singing* are freely substitutable grammatically for the word-groups of which they are constituents. In both cases, then, the italicized word-groups are *headed groups*.

2.4 Non-headed groups, unlike headed groups, can enter into grammatical constructions not open to any single expression within them. No word within the group can substitute for the entire group and make sense, nor can the entire group substitute within the same surrounding context for any one of its constituent parts. Such groups are quite literally non-headed:

> *I saw* a book *of poems.*
> A book *of poems* is what *I saw.*

In these sentences, neither *I* nor *saw* is substitutable for *I saw,* and neither *of* nor *poems* can replace *of poems.* To attempt such substitutions would have these results:

> *I*—a book—*poems.*
> —*Saw* a book *of*—

Alternatively:

I *saw* saw a book of *of poems*.
I *I saw* a book *of poems* poems.

Thus a non-headed group has grammatical functions quite distinct from those of any of its constituent expressions. It may be regarded as representing a chemical combination of its elements, whereas the headed group represents a mechanical combination. Or, to use a linguistic and more appropriate analogy, the non-headed group parallels a word built up with the help of affixes (12.5), while a headed group parallels a compound word (12.4).

2.5 In English, as in most languages, there are many kinds of word-groups classifiable as *headed*. The exact number depends partly upon the exhaustiveness of our analysis and partly upon whether we wish to include the so-called subordinating conjunctions and relative pronouns within the groups they link, or to leave them outside. Since simplicity of analysis is one of our purposes here, it will suffice to be only reasonably exhaustive and to examine the four kinds of headed word-groups that are of basic importance to English grammar and most frequent in occurrence. The first and second, which have the head expression at the end, may be called *tail-head* constructions; the third and fourth, which have their head expressions at the front, may be called *head-tail* constructions. Of the tail-head constructions, the first, already illustrated in 2.3 above, consists of a noun head (i.e., a final word capable of immediately following *the, my, each*) preceded by one, two, or several modifiers (i.e., words in the same group capable of preceding the head):

> *fresh **fruit***
> *nice fresh **fruit***
> *the nice fresh **fruit***
> *all the very nice fresh **fruit***
> *the **fruit***

my fruit
my barn
each little barn
each little cement Vermont barn
The beautiful (are fortunate).
(The book is) *my very own.*
The few (were chosen); *the many* (left behind).
(We told) *each other* (the truth).

These exemplify the *noun-headed word-group.*

2.6 The second kind of headed group, also tail-head in type, has a verb head expression preceded by one, two, or several specialized modifiers (verbal auxiliaries) with or without any inserted adverb:

Trees *can yield* good fruit.
Trees *yield* good fruit.
Trees *may have been yielding* good fruit.
Trees *may* (possibly) *have yielded* good fruit.

These illustrate the *verb-headed word-group.* It is important to notice that the *form* of the head expression may be changed either by adding endings (*yield, yield-ed, yield-ing*), or by replacing the vowel (*sing, sung; feed, fed*), or by both processes (*feel, felt*) in accord with the particular verbal auxiliaries present in the tail. For purposes of grammatical analysis, such *principal parts of the verb* are treated as variants of the simple verb forms (here *yield, sing, feed, feel*) and when substitution is attempted, the appropriate form of the simple verb (6.1–6.2) *must* be chosen:

Trees *can yield* good fruit.
Trees *yield* good fruit.
Trees *will have been yielding* good fruit.
Trees *yield* good fruit.
Trees *may have yielded* good fruit.
Trees *yield* good fruit.
The tree *may have yielded* good fruit.
The tree *yield-s* good fruit.

Otherwise, substitution of the head in its original form for the entire word-group may result in an entirely different grammatical construction:

> Trees *will have been* **yielding** good fruit.
> trees *yielding* good fruit

Here *yielding good fruit* serves as a modifier of trees, not as the verb of the sentence; i.e., we have a different kind of word-group exercising a different grammatical function.

2.7 The third kind of headed word-group, which is of the head-tail type, possesses a front head expression broadly classifiable as *modifier:*

> (a style) **impossible** *to excel*
> (news) **strange** *as death itself*
> (goods) **similar** *to these*
> (funds) **available** *to all*

These examples are typical of what may be called the *modifier-headed word-group*. The substitution of the head for the modifier word-group violates the principle of fixed word order (4.1–4.5) but permits emphatic variation (4.12):

> a style *impossible*
> news *strange*
> goods *similar*
> funds *available*

2.8 Finally, there is the *verbal-headed word-group*, also of the head-tail type, in which the head expression is a verbal, i.e., either the *-ing* form (present participle) or the *to* form (marked infinitive) of a verb. The latter is remarkable as being the only head expression which consists of more than a single word.[3] Examples of verbal-headed word-groups:

---

[3] The *to* infinitive could be itself classified as a non-headed word-group if minute analysis should be required. But notice that the traditional objection to the "split infinitive" implies indivisibility.

Singing songs is fun.
To sing songs is fun.
I like *singing* songs.
I like *to sing* songs.
He drove to New York *singing* songs.
He drove to New York *to sing Mary* songs.

2.9 Two kinds of English non-headed word-groups
have already been illustrated in 2.4 above:

> *of poems*
> *I saw*

In the first of these, a noun, pronoun, or word-group is
hooked onto a preceding word or word-group by means
of a *preposition* (5.5–5.10):

A book
     of
        poems
This book
     of
        mine
A basket
    from
        Naples
The old house
      up
        the street
The cloth
     on
       the table
She was aware
       of
         what he meant.
The car ran
     across
        the curb.

These are examples of the *prepositional word-group*.

2.10 In the second type of non-headed word-group, illustrated above by *I saw,* any single noun, any pronoun, and any type of word-group not verb-headed, modifier-headed, or prepositional is combined with a simple verb or verbal word-group which may itself be followed by other words or word-groups.

I   saw.
The horses   ran.
All the horses   had been running.
Those old trees   may have been yielding fine fruit.
Singing old songs   can often be fun.
(What) he told me   seemed true.

In these, the first constituent is the *subject;* the second constituent, the *predicate* (i.e., assertion). We may consider them, then, as examples of the *subject-predicate word-group.*

2.11 Headed groups may occur with one, two, or several heads. A very common type links individual nouns, pronouns, modifiers or single headed groups (or any combination of these) by means of the words traditionally called *co-ordinating conjunctions* (5.11, 5.26):

> *Jack and Jill* (went up the hill).
> *He and I* (knew the truth).
> (She was) *poor but earnest.*
> *Quick payment or satisfaction* (was needed).
> *Neither food nor money* (was available).

We may conveniently take these as exemplifying the *conjunctional word-group.*

2.12 Thus far, in order to reveal the main lines of analysis pursued here, we have been forced to use a rather cumbersome descriptive terminology. It should now be possible to simplify our terms, using *group* as the equivalent of *word-group* and identifying the headed groups merely by the parts of speech (form classes) which constitute their heads: (1) noun group, (2) verb group, (3) modifier group, (4) verbal group. The total scheme, and the derivation of its parts, may be studied in Fig. 1.

Figure 1

THE PRINCIPAL TYPES OF ENGLISH WORD-GROUPS

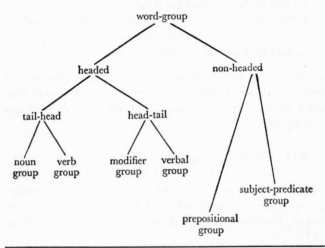

2.13 To understand the structure of English statements, we need to recognize unerringly the four principal types of headed groups (noun groups, verb groups, modifier groups, and verbal groups), the two types of non-headed groups (prepositional groups, subject-predicate groups) and the conjunctional groups. We must also recognize that a group of one type may function as one of the constituents of a group of another type which is itself a constituent of a third, etc. Thus, in the sentence *Jack and Jill had been going to the upland well*(.), the whole sentence is a subject-predicate group which subdivides directly into the subject *Jack and Jill*, itself a conjunctional group, and the predicate *had been going to the upland well*. The latter then subdivides into a verb group *had been going* and a prepositional group *to the upland well* of which the constituent *the upland well* is itself a noun group. Perhaps the point may be made clear if we analyze a rather complicated example:

To sing such songs to a poor old man persuaded of his own approaching death had been a charitable act I had not contemplated.

2.14 Here the entire sentence is a subject-predicate group. On the first level of analysis it consists of a subject *to sing such songs to a poor old man persuaded of his own approaching death* and a predicate *had been a charitable act I had not contemplated.* On the second level of analysis, the subject comprises the verbal group *to sing such songs* and the prepositional group *to a poor old man persuaded of his own approaching death.* The verbal group *to sing such songs* subdivides into the head *to sing* and the noun group *such songs,* with *songs* as its head; the prepositional group *to a poor old man persuaded of his own approaching death* subdivides into the prepositional group *to a poor old man* and a modifier group *persuaded of his own approaching death.* The former consists of the preposition *to* followed by the noun group *a poor old man* with *man* as its head; the latter consists of the modifier head *persuaded* followed by the prepositional group *of his own approaching death* which itself comprises the preposition *of* and the noun group *his own approaching death* with *death* as its head. In similar fashion, the predicate *had been a charitable act I had not contemplated* is first analyzed into the verb group *had been* with *been* as the head, and the complement (3.14) *a charitable act I had not contemplated.* This in turn subdivides into a noun group *a charitable act* with *act* as its head and a subject-predicate group *I had not contemplated.* Finally, the constituents of *I had not contemplated* are its subject *I* and its predicate, the verb group *had not contemplated,* with *contemplated* as its head. The results of this extended analysis and the method of analyzing the various levels of constituents by which it was accomplished are illustrated in Fig. 2.

2.15 The value of such analyses in depth is that they reveal the Chinese-puzzle intricacy of English utterances without confusing the various levels of grammatical structure. Yet merely to break down the statement into its more obvious groups and to recognize their types is often sufficient to reveal its major grammatical dynamics:

<table>
<tr><td>conj. gr.</td><td>vb. gr.</td><td>prep. gr.</td></tr>
<tr><td>*Jack and Jill*</td><td>*had been going*</td><td>*to the upland well.*</td></tr>
</table>

<table>
<tr><td>vbl. gr.</td><td>prep. gr.</td></tr>
<tr><td>*To sing such songs*</td><td>*to a poor old man*</td></tr>
</table>

<table>
<tr><td>mod. gr.</td><td>vb. gr.</td></tr>
<tr><td>*persuaded of his own approaching death*</td><td>*had been*</td></tr>
</table>

<table>
<tr><td>n. gr.</td><td>subj.-pred. gr.</td></tr>
<tr><td>*a charitable act*</td><td>*I had not contemplated.*</td></tr>
</table>

The striking thing here is that the breakdown is not usually made by scrutinizing the constituent elements of each of the groups. Most native speakers of English perform the operation almost unconsciously by slowing down their articulation and taking note of the natural rhythm patterns of the statement. Rhythm, in fact, lies at the very heart of English grammatical structure.

2.16 The three factors which determine the rhythm patterns of our language are (1) relative voice loudness or *stress,* (2) relative voice frequency or *tone,* (3) *interruption* of normal transition between contiguous speech sounds (*juncture*), usually followed in slow speech or slow reading by pause at points of grammatical

Figure 2

ANALYSIS BY WORD-GROUP CONSTITUENTS

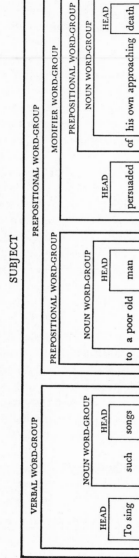

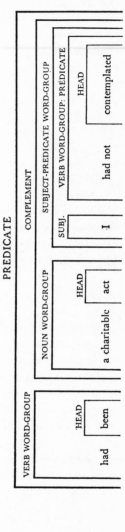

cleavage. Since these three configurational factors occur in close association, there seems little doubt that most of us tend to interpret the grammatical situation not through all of them but by one or another of them to which we may be specially attuned. Some persons very susceptible to variations of *tone* are little susceptible to variations of *stress*. Some persons are quick to notice the combination of sound prolongation, voice fade versus abrupt voice cutoff, and tonal rise or fall before juncture points; others find them difficult to perceive. In the long run, it makes little difference. Every normal speaker of English signals the grammatical structure of his statements by the use of *tone, stress,* and what is nowadays called *juncture*. Every normal hearer responds sufficiently to his signals to understand that grammatical structure. In the written language, the ability to reconstruct the grammatical signals that a speaker might use, and that the writer presupposes, may mark a reader's understanding or lack of understanding of what has been written down. Since the main function of tone variation is to signal for specific types of attentiveness or response (3.6–3.8) at juncture before breath intake, viz. at the ends of sentences, discussion of it will be deferred until the next chapter. Here we shall be concerned with *stress* and *juncture* as they occur within the limits of the sentence span. We should understand, however, that the following remarks apply particularly to the slowed-down articulation tempo or reading perception which is basic to the analysis of written English grammatical structure.

2.17 In spoken English, the placement of stress is of primary grammatical importance. Not only does it distinguish between words otherwise of identical speech-sound shape such as *belów* and *bíllow;* it has other and much more varied functions:

a. Stress placement differentiates two-syllable nouns from their corresponding verbs:

NOUNS (falling stress pattern)	VERBS (rising stress pattern)
ˢ↘ address	↗ˢ address
ˢ↘ conflict	↗ˢ conflict
ˢ↘ contract	↗ˢ contract
ˢ↘ converse	↗ˢ converse
ˢ↘ convict	↗ˢ convict
ˢ↘ impact	↗ˢ impact
ˢ↘ import	↗ˢ import
ˢ↘ imprint	↗ˢ imprint
ˢ↘ increase	↗ˢ increase
ˢ↘ inlay	↗ˢ inlay
ˢ↘ insert	↗ˢ insert
ˢ↘ insult	↗ˢ insult
ˢ↘ project	↗ˢ project
ˢ↘ rebel	↗ˢ rebel
ˢ↘ transfer	↗ˢ transfer

Similarly:

a ˢ↘ *cutback* in prices	I *cut ↗ˢ back* my stocks.
a ˢ↘ *markup* in clothing	I *mark ↗ˢ up* my prices.
a ˢ↘ *breakthrough* of tanks	The tanks *break ↗ through* ˢ.

b. Stress placement distinguishes compound words from noun groups:

| COMPOUND WORD | NOUN GROUP |
| (falling stress pattern) | (rising stress pattern) |

white͟wash   `s ↘`

a white wash   `↗ s`

black͟bird   `s ↘`

a black bird   `↗ s`

club͟house   `s ↘`

a club house   `↗ s`

ice͟cream (some speakers)   `s ↘`

ice cream (some speakers)   `↗ s`

2.18   What has happened in the last group of examples is of particular interest. English is constantly forming words for new referents by combining
words already in the language. Some of these *compounds,*
as they are called, may be deliberately put together (e.g.,
folklore); most of them evolve from noun groups—groups
constantly repeated as the referents which they symbolize
come more and more into familiar use. In the course of
repetition, something very significant happens: the point
at which one applies maximum loudness (*maximum
stress*) shifts from the last word or from some syllable of
the last word to the preceding modifier or to some syllable of the preceding modifier. The noun group becomes
a compound word. When Robert Fulton, in 1807, in-
stalled a steam engine in a boat and successfully navi-
gated it from New York to Albany, people referred to his
contraption as a *steam ↗ boat.* Later, as such boats became common in American waters, they were known as
steam↘boats. In England, where our favorite dessert is not
as popular as here, it is still referred to by the noun group
ice↗ cream; we often call it *icecream↘.* The same process of
shift in stress placing has been responsible for the formation of many other compound words: *whitewash↘* from

white ˊwash, ˋblackbird from *blackˊbird, ˋclubhouse* from
ˊclub house, atomˋbomb from *atomˊbomb,* and so forth.

2.19 In all the examples given above, the writing of the constituent elements as one word or two plainly shows which are to be regarded as compounds and which as noun groups. Modern English, however, possesses very many compounds so recently formed that their components are still written as separate words. Such are *teleˋphone stand, ˋmessenger boy,* and *inˋsurance agent,* all three of which are plainly indicated as compound words by their falling stress patterns. Such, for that matter, are the terms *comˋpound word* and *ˋstress patterns* as used in the last sentence. Moreover, a sequence of words may be used in some contexts as a group, in others as a compound word. Just as one may speak to a *ˋFrenchman* (compound) or notice a *Frenchˊman* (noun group), one may be fond of a *ˋFrench girl* (compound) or swim with a little *Frenchˊgirl* (noun group).

2.20 But our use of stress far exceeds the situations already examined. English, unlike many other Western languages, can use words of the same phonetic shape in various grammatical frames with varied grammatical functions. Thus in the frames,

> *He jumped —— the window.*
> *My orders came ——.*
> *The —— train was halted.*

the insertion of *through* will automatically distinguish the three grammatical functions of that word as preposition, directive adverb, and modifier. Similarly:

I had to *cut* the grass.   (*cut* as verb)
The *cut* in my hand healed.   (*cut* as noun)
I bandaged my *cut* hand.   (*cut* as modifier)

The *back* of the garden was beautiful. (*back* as noun)
We always *back* the boat into the lake. (*back* as verb)
We gave the woman her purse *back*.   (*back* as adverb)

As we read these examples aloud, we immediately notice that the various grammatical functions of *through, cut,* and *back* are differentiated not only by their relative *positions* in the statements but also by the *relative degrees of loudness applied to them by virtue of those positions.* Here, then, is a most important feature of English.

2.21 Quite possibly we may interpret this feature chiefly in terms of the placing of maximum loudness:

I had to *cut* the ⟋ˢ grass.

The ˢ⟍ *cut* in my hand healed. ˢ

I bandaged ˢ⟍ my *cut* ⟋ˢ hand.

Even in the following crucial instances, that may be all that is needed:

a *light͡house͏keeper* ˢ⟍ (one who keeps a lighthouse)

a *light house͏keeper* ˢ⟍ (one who does light housekeeping)

the *long͏house* ˢ⟍ (Indian council hall)

the *long house* ⟋ˢ (house which is long)

For purposes of purely grammatical analysis, therefore, it may prove sufficient to locate maximum stresses in sevtences and word-groups and temporarily put aside other considerations, especially if we find that the perception of detailed stress and juncture differences proves troublesome:

    Poor John   *had been given*   *expensive presents.*

    The farmer   *was bricking*   *up the chimney.*

    The farmer   *was bricking up*   *the chimney.*

To locate points of maximum stress and to recognize that internal juncture points will occur after *any single maximally stressed word or after the last maximally stressed word of any word-group* is to possess an easy clue—and one shared by all normal users of English—to the grammatical segmentation of sentences.

2.22 How much further than this we need to go for our present purposes it is difficult to say. Yet it is obvious that the grammatical differences we have been considering involve not only contrasts of grammatical structure but also differences of meaning not adequately covered by the simple contrast of stressed with stressless syllables. The point becomes quite clear when we extend the scope of some of our examples:

the *longhouse* (Indian council hall)

the *long house* (a house which is long)

the *Long house* (the house of the Long family)

a *lighthousekeeper* (one who keeps a lighthouse)

a *light housekeeper* (one who does light housekeeping)

a *light housekeeper* (a housekeeper who is not brunette, or, alternately, not heavy)

In these, although stress placement is sufficient to discriminate the compounds from the noun groups, it is not sufficient to discriminate each pair of noun groups from each other. *House* in *Long house* and *house* in *long house* differ in the degree of stress applied to them; so also with the *light* of *light housekeeper* (a light housekeeper who is not brunette or heavy) as compared with the *light* of *light housekeeper* (one who does light housekeeping). Here, apparently, we are dealing with the same phenomenon as appears in the distinction between *cut* as noun, verb, and modifier in 2.20 above.

2.23 The total stress system of spoken English, in fact, involves not only the contrast between rising and falling stress patterns but also the application of four degrees of stress to various syllables. These degrees may be characterized as *maximum stress* ($\diagup$), *major stress* ($\wedge$), *minor stress* ($\diagdown$), and *minimum stress* ($\smile$).[4] All four of these may be heard in *lighthousekeeper* and also in our *long house* examples:

$$\overset{\smile}{\text{the}} \overset{\diagup}{\text{long}}\overset{\diagdown}{\text{house}}$$

$$\overset{\smile}{\text{the}} \overset{\diagdown}{\text{long}}\overset{\diagup}{\text{house}}$$

$$\overset{\smile}{\text{the}} \overset{\diagup}{\text{Long}}\overset{\wedge}{\text{house}}$$

Similarly in:

$$\overset{\smile}{\text{I}}\overset{\diagdown}{\text{had}} \text{ to } \overset{\smile}{\text{cut}}\overset{\wedge}{} \text{ the } \overset{\smile}{\text{grass}}\overset{\diagup}{.}$$

$$\overset{\smile}{\text{the}} \overset{\diagup}{\text{cut}}\overset{\diagdown}{} \text{ in } \overset{\smile}{\text{my}} \overset{\diagup}{\text{hand}}$$

$$\overset{\smile}{\text{my}} \overset{\diagdown}{\text{cut}} \overset{\diagup}{\text{hand}}$$

Notice, however, that since the discrimination of stress levels varies sharply from human being to human being,

---

[4] This terminology is chosen in order to allow for the practical definition of a syllable as "a stretch of speech-sounds over which a stress extends."

some of us may have difficulty in differentiating between
the major stress (∧) and the maximum stress (/), or between the minor stress (\) and the minimal stress (∪)
even though we may be using all four stresses in our
actual speaking.

2.24 Closely associated with the occurrences of the
four degrees of stress are two types of *juncture*,
i.e., of interruption of the normal transition between
speech-sounds:

a. **Open juncture** (usually marked + by linguists) **is**
essentially a gradual fade-off of the voice, often accompanied by prolongation of the last speech-sounds preceding it and sometimes followed by pause (especially in
reading poetry). It is used by all speakers between contiguous syllables neither of which has minimum stress,
and by some speakers after a minimally stressed syllable
also:

/ + \ + ∧ ∪
lighthousekeeper (keeper of a lighthouse)

\ + / + ∧ ∪
light housekeeper (one who does light housekeeping)

/ + ∧ + \ ∪
light housekeeper (housekeeper not heavy or brunette)

/ + \
longhouse (Indian council hall)

\ + /
long house

/ + ∧
Long house

b. **Internal grammatical juncture** (symbolized in this
book by spacing or the comma) combines distinct prolongation of the last speech-sounds preceding it with
abrupt voice cutoff at the end of the final sound. In slow-
tempo reading or speaking it is often followed by a pause.
It may occur after any single stressed word or word-group
when either is a distinct grammatical constituent of a
sentence:

The fármer   was brícking   up the chímney.

The fármer   was brìcking úp   the chímney.

Jóhn   had been gíving   expènsive présents

to the yòung láy.

When I percêived the trúth,   I was disgústed.

2.25 Both open juncture and internal grammatical juncture are closely associated with the placing of stresses. Thus stress and juncture work together in signaling the grammatical structure of statements. What happens when we use them to discriminate grammatical function is that we respond to various contrastive rhythmical patterns based upon various arrangements of the two factors. It is stress-juncture rhythm which gives us our most direct clue to grammatical arrangement and permits us to subdivide statements into their constituent words and word-groups. Rhythm is the first essential of the structural essentials of English—the first and basic device of modern English grammar.

3 | Sentences

3.1 As we have seen, word-groups may occur either as units in sequences of larger statements or they may occur as statements in themselves. In the latter case, their ending points will be marked by that interruption between the normal transition from one speech-sound to the next that we have called *juncture*—in this case juncture preceding the breath intake that inaugurates the beginning of the next statement. From the standpoint of speech, therefore, a sentence could be scientifically defined as *any stretch of utterance between breath intakes.* Yet, since breathing is so automatic a process that intake or output of the breath is probably something below the threshold of consciousness, we seem to recognize the transition from one sentence to another by the distinctive features of the final junctures of each of our statements. These are (1) prolongation of the last speech-sounds of a statement; (2) gradual voice fade, or, alternatively, abrupt voice cutoff; and (3) significant change in the tone of the voice. In fast speaking these are often, and in slow speaking always, followed by a breathing pause. Since the most immediately perceptible of these phenomena are the tone change and the following pause, it is practical to define the spoken sentence as *a word-group, or more seldom a single word, the end of which* *is marked by a final tone-pause pattern.* A written sentence can then be defined as *a word-group or word with end punctuation intended to symbolize a final tone-pause pattern.*

3.2 Actually, the punctuation marks now used in English record final tone-pause patterns rather imperfectly (10.1): the period, for a fall from high to the lowest tone (with voice fade) preceding breathing pause; the question mark, either for this same pattern or, in statements without an interrogative word or without interrogative word order, for a rising high tone (with abrupt voice cutoff) preceding breathing pause; the exclamation mark for unusual tonal fall, rise, or level (often combined with exaggerated voice fade or voice cutoff), together with unusually vehement or non-vehement qualities of the voice preceding breathing pause (1.2). All of these are in direct contrast with the non-final juncture *(internal grammatical juncture,* see 2.24) marked in speech by level tone and lack of breath intake (also by speech-sound prolongation and abrupt voice cutoff), and in writing either left unpunctuated or, in certain circumstances (10.8), punctuated by the comma. Other non-final punctuation marks, the colon, the semicolon, and the dash, which are dissociated from the realities of tone-pause patterns, indicate various kinds of linkage between sentences, word-groups, and single words, and are best regarded as symbolic conjunctions (10.3).

3.3 English sentences, then, are not sentences merely by virtue of the kinds of words or word-groups they contain; they are sentences because they end with one or other of the final tone-pause patterns characteristic of the English language. It is the presence of tone pause, whether actual or symbolized by punctuation, which determines what is and what is not a sentence. The same word-group, therefore, may occur as a sentence of this or that type, or as a sub-sentence unit:

> *Her cheeks*   *paled.*
> *Her cheeks*   *paled?*
> *Her cheeks*   *paled!*
> *It was obvious*   *her cheeks paled.*
> *Her cheeks paled*   *and*   *her breath failed.*

In either case, it is the presence or absence of preceding or following tone-pause patterns, either actual or symbolized by punctuation, which decides the question:

> It was obvious   *her cheeks paled.*
> It was obvious.   *Her cheeks paled.*

3.4 Ever since we learned to listen and talk, we have been making use of variations in *tone level*. Yet most of us never knew what we were doing or why. The easiest way to understand the part played by tone in English is as follows. Tone depends upon the vibrational frequencies put into the pronunciation of vowels and certain consonants: the higher the frequency, the higher the tone of voice; the lower the frequency, the lower the tone of voice. All of us have a *normal* tone on which we pronounce most of the words and syllables of utterances. From time to time, however, our voices rise *above* the normal tone level as we pronounce certain syllables; at other times, they drop *below* our normal tone level. Every time we depart from the normal tone level, either by rising above it or falling below it, we indicate something significant about what we are saying. This something is our attitude of mind to what we are saying. *Tone of voice reflects psychological tone.*

3.5 Since psychological attitudes may be highly complex, many things expressed by changes of tone lie outside the province of grammar. Think, for instance, of the serious, humorous, sardonic, ironic, or affectionate intonations applicable to *Oh yeah*(!) or *You silly fool*(!) or to *He's a good scholar*(.), *He's a good scholar*. . . . The differences between these intonations, seconded by the exact quality of the voice, are masked rather than revealed by the punctuation mark. Fortunately for communication, the important grammatical indications of tone pattern are neither particularly varied nor particularly subtle. They center around the simple contrast between a *high falling tone pattern* and a *high rising tone pattern,* just as stress contrasts center around a rising versus a falling stress pattern (2.17–2.18).

3.6 The significant tone levels of English are four: *highest* (hh), *high* (h), *normal* (n), and *low* (l). Of these, the highest level (hh) seems to be used interchangeably with the high level (h), especially in utterances charged with emotion. The grammatical meaning of the high tones is "high attention demanded." That of the normal tone is "normal attention demanded." That of the low tone is "low attention demanded." Thus a movement from one tone to another has necessarily great grammatical significance.

3.7 The commonest English tone pattern involves a sharp fall from one of the high tones (usually from h) to the low tone of the voice. This very important pattern is used in combination with final pause (i.e., pause before breath intake) with the general meaning "attention can now sink below normal" or "finality" as follows:

a. On single words used as individual declarative utterances:

h—l	h—l	h———l	h———l
Bed.	*Three.*	*Typewriter.*	*Blackbird.*

b. On the last stressed word of any word-group used as a sentence of a declarative nature:

                        h—l   h—l
I bought some books.   *I went to a movie.*
                        h—l——
The general reviewed our regiment.

h——l——
The more, the merrier.   h——l
The sooner, the better.

h————l
John was punished for all his misdemeanors.

c. Usually, on a single interrogative word or on the last stressed word of a question introduced by an interrogative word:

h————l   h———l   h——l   h——l
Where?   *When?*   *Why?*   *Where was he first?*

h——l——
How was the movie?

This final tone pattern is characterized also by a gradual fade of the voice at the point of tone change and, in slow-tempo speech, is followed by breath-intake pause.

3.8   The second common English final tone pattern involves rising higher tone (usually h ⌣↗) commencing on the last stressed syllable of a sentence. With the general meanings "something worth attention follows," or "here is something surprising," or "answer expected," this pattern occurs as follows:

a. On the stressed final syllables of questions not introduced by interrogative words:

h ⌣↗
You brought me some books?

h   ⌣↗
The general reviewed our regiment?

h ⌣↗
They went to the theater?

b. On single interrogative words or on the last stressed syllables of question sentences introduced by such words when either surprise or call for a repeated answer is to be signaled:

h ⌣↗   h ⌣↗   h ⌣↗   h ⌣↗
Where?   *When?*   *Why?*   *Where was the fire?*

c. Often, on the stressed words of series statements:

h ⌣ h⌣ h ⌣ h⌣   h–l
One, two, three, four, and five.

n   h⌣   h ⌣ h   ⌣ n h–l
I took a gun, a kettle, a blanket-roll, and a tent.

This tone pattern is characterized also by abrupt cut-off of the voice at the end of the word and, in the slow-tempo speech proper to grammatical analysis, is followed by breath-intake pause.

3.9 The third common tone pattern occurs at internal grammatical juncture (2.24b) and is probably non-distinctive.[1] It involves for the most part normal tone level on both sides of an internal grammatical juncture usually after a fall from high tone at the syllable division of a compound or during the vowel of a single syllable word:

n   h—n   n   h—l
The commander   had given the lady   a present.
n   h—n   n   h—l
Going down the river,   I saw Cairo on the right.

In the last example, read aloud at the slow tempo necessary for grammatical analysis, the internal grammatical juncture is backed by a pause.

3.10 To tell what is and what is not a sentence, the best method is to make oneself familiar with the tone patterns schematized above. To do that successfully is to broaden one's comprehension of what an English sentence is and does. Remember: *English sentences are not sentences by virtue of the kinds of constructions they embody or the kinds of words they contain; they are sentences because they possess one or other of the final tone-pause patterns characteristic of the language.* In practice, the implications of this statement are much easier than they seem to be. Very little practice is needed

[1] It is sometimes used before final juncture to express derogation.
                      h–l   h——n
Contrast: *He's a good scholar* with *He's a good scholar.*

to discriminate the final high rising tone pattern from the final high-low tone pattern or either from the internal level tone-pause pattern. Moreover, since the great majority of English written sentences are declarative, the one tone-pause pattern which we must learn to recognize is that distinguished by high-low (h–l) tone. The first step towards comprehension of sentences is to recognize it unerringly. The rest is largely bookkeeping.

3.11 Since for most of us the notion of juncture and the tone-pause and stress-juncture patterns by which it is described in this book may be somewhat novel, we may as well summarize at this point the distinguishing features which mark each one of the four phenomena (Fig. 3).

Figure 3

THE SEGMENT MARKERS (JUNCTURE SITUATIONS) OF ENGLISH

	FINAL		NON-FINAL	
	Declarative-inter-rogative (3.7)	*Ques-tional* (3.8)	*Internal grammatical* (2.24–2.25)	*Open* (2.24–2.25)
DISTINGUISHING FEATURES:				
1. Prolongation of preceding sounds	plus	plus	plus	neutral
2. Gradual voice fade	plus	minus	minus	plus
3. Abrupt voice cut-off	minus	plus	plus	minus
4. Tone rise	minus	plus	neutral	minus
5. Tone fall	plus	minus	neutral	neutral
6. Following pause in slow-speech tempo	plus	plus	plus	neutral
MAIN DISTINGUISHING FEATURE:	tone-fall	tone-rise	prolongation	gradual voice fade

3.12 In all languages, the principal types of sentences seem to be based on a very limited number of the types of word-groups. In written English, the *subject-predicate sentence,* which is the subject-predicate word-group accompanied by the declarative high-low tone-pause pattern, is so overwhelmingly popular that it has almost banished other sentence types from educational recognition. Yet other types, whether of an infrequent or minor kind, commonly occur in speech and can play an important stylistic role in dialogue, poetry, and dynamic narrative. They seldom appear in non-conversational writing:

a. *Question sentences:*

> Did she say that?
> She said that?
> Did you go to the theater?

b. *Equational sentences:*

> The more, the merrier.
> Like father, like son.
> Fine young girl, that!

c. *Completive sentences:*

(Are you coming along?) Whenever you're ready.
(When shall we leave?) This afternoon.

d. *Exclamatory sentences:*

> Go away!

e. *Reportage sentences:*

"Tact. By the Police Force." Such were the words of the accused.

"Age fifty. Middle height. Fair skin when washed—which he wasn't."

All these are useful and reputable sentences. None of them is to be stigmatized, as so often they are stigmatized, as *sentence fragments*. For all that, the subject-predicate sentence is *the* sentence of written English. Its grammatical structure accounts for almost all the English grammar that is practically useful to a writer of the language. Understand this structure, this grammar, and you will have the grammatical dynamics of the language well within your grasp.

3.13 Real-life situations expressed through the subject-predicate sentence involve relations established between two or more persons, things, qualities, ideas, and so forth. To convey such situations in words, some device or devices will be needed by which to state the irreducible minimum of grammatical information: (1) the names of whatever may be involved, and (2) the identifying attributes of whatever may be involved. In contemporary English, both these pieces of information are expressed chiefly by the grammatical device of *fixed word order*—a device itself based firmly on what may be reckoned the foundation principle of our grammatical system: *essential sentence elements occupy fixed positions; less essential elements tend to be movable.* Yet neither this principle nor the word-order device based on it could operate very successfully without the functional stress-juncture patterns of our language (2.19–2.21).

3.14 The subject-predicate sentence comprises a noun, pronoun, or any word-group not verb-headed or modifier-headed or prepositional, coupled with a verb or verb word-group bearing a final tone-pause pattern. In English, we recognize the primary constituents of such a sentence mainly by the fixed positions they fill, the first position being reserved for the subject and the second for the predicate. The simplest form of the sentence—that which consists simply of subject and of verb or verb group predicate—may be called SENTENCE SITUATION I:

SUBJECT	PREDICATE
1	2
Jesus	wept.
He	cried.
Boys	yell.
All the good men	had been fighting.
What he had attempted	had failed.
To sing such songs as this	could help.

These, however, reflect a linguistic situation so simple that it occurs comparatively rarely. In many subject-predicate sentences, the predicate contains two constituents, first a verb or verb word-group, and then a *complement* (i.e., completer). The purpose of the complement is to bring into the scope of the sentence situation something not referred to in the subject. The presence of a complement characterizes SENTENCE SITUATION II:

SUBJECT	PREDICATE	
1	2 *Verb*	3 *Complement*
Germany	defeated	France.
The President	dominated	Congress.
The matter	slipped	his memory.
All the men	talked	shop.
It	was raining	cats and dogs.
To say good-bye	is	to die a little.
Jackson	had said	he needed arms.
All the detectives	reported	what they had seen.
They	could be	themselves.
The sales manager	became	secretary.
The house	seemed	broken down.

Although exhaustive analysis might discriminate several types of verbs and complements among these examples, the word-order pattern (1, 2, 3) is the same for all. Syntactically, therefore, they represent the same sentence

situation. That is true even when movable verb modifiers (4.7) are inserted between the verb position and
the complement position:

1	2	3
The house	*had been* (already)	*on fire.*

1	2	3
The house	*was* (, as I have said,)	*on fire.*

3.15 In many sentences, the predicate includes two
complements, one of which in rapid speech is
tied to the tone level of the verb or verb word-group.
This, whatever its detailed grammatical status, may be
called the *inner complement* while the other, in view of
its position, may be called the *outer complement*. A sentence with two complements represents SENTENCE SITUA-
TION III.

SUBJECT	PREDICATE		
1	2 *Verb*	3 *Inner Complement*	4 *Outer Complement*
The reporter	gave	the lady	a present.
Father	sent	Mary	money.
Indifference	lost	England	America.
Students	called	their professor	names.
Parliament	had made	Henry Bolingbroke	king.
Stony paths	were making	our way	a horror.
Tom Sawyer	painted	the fence	white.
We	found	the house	broken down.
The captain	had wanted	his aide	to examine the matter.
The sailor	promised	himself	a treat.
All the men	considered	their cause	ruined.

Here again, as in SENTENCE SITUATION II, further analysis
and further consideration of stress and tone-pause patterns would reveal marked grammatical differences between the kinds of verbs and kinds of complements
that appear in these and other possible examples. Yet

because the word-order pattern is constant, we are not at all conscious of any such differences and distinctions. *For all practical purposes, the present analysis is enough* (but see 4.10).

3.16 SENTENCE SITUATIONS I, II, and III clearly show the structural skeleton of fixed word order which supports the flesh of the English subject-predicate sentence. It can be thus briefly described:

In the subject-predicate sentence, the subject, the verb, any inner complement, and any outer complement normally occur in a fixed 1, 2, 3, 4 order.

This then is the second and, in many respects, the least understood principle of modern English grammatical structure.

4 Modification and shift of emphasis

4.1 The complements of a predicate restrict the range of application of the verb. Thus, in a very real sense, they are *modifiers*. But the modification of sentence elements does not stop short with the complements. Neither human communication nor the life occurrences it reflects are often uncomplicated, and any key word in a fixed word-order slot may need to carry its own modification. This may be accomplished by the use of single word modifiers, or word-group modifiers, or both.

4.2 In positions 1, 3, and 4, within the sentence, *individual* words used as word modifiers, whether singly or in series, tend to occur before the word that they modify. Such modifiers, therefore, build up noun word-groups of which the modified word is the head:

1	2	3
*A handsome **reporter***	gave	*a young **lady***
4		
*valuable **presents.***		

> ¹   ²
> *All the young **reporters***   gave
> ³
> *a most charming young **lady***
> ⁴
> *certain very valuable **books.***

In word-order position 2, the specialized modifiers called
auxiliaries (verbal helpers) always precede the modified
verb, building up verb word-groups of which the verb is
the head:

> ¹   ²   ³   ⁴
> A reporter   *had been **giving***   a lady   the books.
> ¹   ²   ³
> A reporter   *had been about to **give***   a lady
> ⁴
> the books.

4.3   *Word-groups* used as word modifiers follow the
word that they modify:

> ¹   ²
> A ***reporter*** *on the News*   gave
> ³
> the ***lady*** *I have mentioned*
> ⁴
> ***books*** *of accumulated press clippings.*
> ¹   ²
> The ***reporter*** *I have been consulting*   gave
> ³
> the ***lady*** *from Duluth*
> ⁴
> the ***books*** *I have just mentioned.*
> ¹
> A ***reporter*** *persuaded of his own irresistible charm*
> ²   ³
> gave   a ***lady*** *convinced of hers*
> ⁴
> various ***books*** *of verse.*
> ¹   ²
> The ***reporter***, *a very charming person,*   gave
> ³   ⁴
> this ***lady***, *a young debutante,*   various ***books*** *of verse.*

4.4   Although word-group modifiers are usually of the non-headed types, headed groups, as can be seen above, are not infrequent in positions 1, 3, and 4. In speech, noun groups (*appositives,* repeaters) are separated from the word they modify by the internal grammatical juncture; in writing, by the comma that is its symbol (2.24). The presence of this juncture between the word modified and the modifying word-group marks the latter as *non-restrictive;* its absence marks it as *restrictive.* As used in modification, noun groups seem always to be non-restrictive; modifier and subject-predicate groups may be either restrictive or non-restrictive; prepositional groups are usually—not always—restrictive. But today a new factor seems to be entering the situation: the use of such groups as (*the man*) *I have just mentioned,* (*the girl*) *I was speaking about,* (*the reporter*) *persuaded of his own charm* instead of the older and fuller forms (*the man*) *whom I have just mentioned,* (*the girl*) *about whom I was speaking,* (*the reporter*) *who was persuaded of his own charms.* Among certain modern writers, groups with *who(m), which, that,* seem to be used as automatically non-restrictive when immediately following the word modified, those without *who(m), which, that* being automatically restrictive. A new method of expressing the grammatical distinction of restriction may be arising.

4.5   In 3.13, the second major grammatical device was stated:

In the subject-predicate sentence, the subject, the verb, any inner complement, and any outer complement occur in a fixed 1, 2, 3, 4 order.

To this we may add a third device, almost equally important:

Single word modifiers normally precede, and word-group modifiers normally follow, the words they modify.

In these two simple principles is embodied the essential core of English grammatical structure. To understand them and to make practical use of them is to take the first long stride towards mastery of effective written English. Once they are thoroughly understood, the structure of a sentence even as badly complicated and undesirably over-modified as the following will become immediately transparent:

Very nearly all of the many fine young reporters I spoke
to in the offices of the News at Duluth, a group of
energetic young men, had been going to give
the very pretty little debutante girl from Indianapolis,
who was more than a little persuaded of her own
charms, magnificent presents of orchids from Java.

4.6 So far we have been concerned with the *must* elements of sentences. In addition to these, many English sentences possess less essential elements— a kind of linguistic envelope for the *must* elements— which provide a spatial, temporal, emotional, and intensity setting appropriate to the sentence situation. These are often thought of as *adverbial modifiers,* considered as reacting on the verb and its expansions. From the standpoint of word order, the important thing about them is that their positions are relatively unfixed; they are the only really movable elements that English sentences possess. Thus they exemplify to a remarkable degree the basic principle already mentioned in 3.13:

The essential elements occupy fixed positions; less essential elements tend to be movable.

Since the important thing about these modifiers is that they *are* movable, and since the term *adverb* is commonly used to cover several classes of words quite different in function, we shall call these modifiers *movable modifiers*.

4.7 Movable modifiers include single words, headed groups, and non-headed groups. According to the positions in which they may be inserted, they may be further classified as follows:

a. **Directives** (spatial adverbs, see 5.6), such as *in, out, under, over, back, home,* etc., normally occur *after* the verb. When only a single complement is present, they may occur immediately after the verb or immediately after the complement (i.e., after positions 2 or 3):

	2		3
The reporter	gave	*back*	the books.

	2	3	
The reporter	gave	the books	*back*.

When an inner and an outer complement are present in a sentence, *directives* may occur either before them, or between them, or immediately after the outer complement (i.e., after positions 2, 3 or 4):

	2	3	4
The reporter	gave *back*	the lady	her books.
The reporter	gave	the lady *back*	her books.
The reporter	gave	the lady	her books *back*.

That *directives* are very intimately linked with their verbs is proved by the noun compounds into which they enter: *cutback* (v. *cut back*), *come-on* (v. *come on*), *breakthrough* (v. *break through*), etc.[1] Consequently, they precede all other movable modifiers placed after the verb:

1	2	3	4
The reporter	gave	the lady	her books

back at noon today.

[1] If directives could not shift in position after the verb, another type of word-group, verb plus directive (complex verb), might be established.

b. **Qualifiers** (qualifying adverbs), which include modifiers ending in *-ly,* and such other words as *here, now, then, there, next, often, later, still, almost, sometimes,* differ from directives in that they can be inserted before the verb as well as after it. If the verb is a single word they may be placed before the subject or between the subject and the verb (that is, before position 1 or between positions 1 and 2):

Presumably the reporter[1] gave[2] the lady[3] books.[4]

Next the reporter[1] gave[2] the lady[3] books.[4]

The reporter *presumably*[1] gave[2] the lady[3] books.[4]

The reporter *next*[1] gave[2] the lady[3] books.[4]

In speech, but more rarely in writing, they are often placed at the end of the sentence:

The reporter[1] gave[2] the lady[3] books[4] *presumably.*

The reporter[1] gave[2] the lady[3] books[4] *then.*

If position 2 (the verb position) is filled by a verb-headed word-group qualifiers may either precede it or be placed after its first element:

The reporter *presumably*[1] was giving[2] a lady[3] books.[4]

The reporter[1] was *presumably* giving[2] a lady[3] books.[4]

The reporter[1] had *still* been about to give[2] a lady[3] books.[4]

c. **Group qualifiers** commonly appear at the end of the sentence, but they may precede position 1 or be placed between positions 1 and 2:

1	2	3	4
The reporter	gave	the lady	books *on the way*

home.

1	2	3	4
The reporter	gave	the lady	books *to show ap-*

preciation.

1	2	3	4
The reporter	gave	the lady	books *when he re-*

turned.

On the way home ⎫
To show appreciation, ⎭ the reporter¹ gave² the lady³ books⁴.

The reporter¹, *when he returned,* gave² the lady³ books⁴.

Needless to say, any sentence may contain various kinds of movable modifiers in any or all of the available positions:

When he returned, the reporter¹ had *presumably* given² the lady³ these books⁴ *back in that Italian garden.*

The tremendous flexibility of the English sentence is largely made possible by the various positions open to the movable modifiers.

4.8 The fixed patterns of word order in English have one practical disadvantage: they limit the opportunity to shift the emphasis from one part of a sentence to another merely by changing the order of the words. Few writers of modern prose would be daring enough to follow the example set by Dickens' famous sentence:

3   1   2   3   1   2
Talent, Mr. Micawber has; money, Mr. Micawber has not.

Even such milder inversions of the normal order as *Came the dawn!* and *Had she been there, she would have been safe*(.) are felt to be strange, the former as a Hollywood cliché and the latter as belonging to the nineteenth rather than to the twentieth century. In expository writing, however, occasional use of the inverted complement marks the continuity of thought in contiguous sentences:

1   2   3
Certain persons resisted his military regime.

3   1   2   4
Those persons he called "pseudo-internationalists."

Similarly, for purposes of enumeration, a qualifier is sometimes placed at the beginning of the sentence with the verb immediately following:

2   1
Next comes the logical figure termed the syllogism.

In story-telling technique, a directive and verb sometimes occur in this same order:

2   1
Back ran the bear to his mother.

Yet, in general, sentence emphasis is now varied not by changing the order of the words but by using special constructions. Just as we possess a grammatical device of fixed word order, we also possess devices for shifting emphasis from one element of the standard written sentence to another.

   4.9 Special emphasis may be thrown upon the subject (position 1) by placing before it either of the two introductory formulae *it is* (*was*), *there is* (*are, was, were*) and by turning the following part of the sen-

tence into a modifying subject-predicate group preceded
by the linking words *who(m), which* or *that:*

> *It was* the reporter *who* gave the lady books.
> *There was* a reporter *that* gave the lady books.

In all fairness, we should note that this is only one of the
astonishing array of *it is, there is* constructions in English.

4.10 Special emphasis may be thrown upon the
words forming the inner and outer comple-
ments of the standard sentence (positions 3 and 4) by the
use of the so-called *passive construction.* In this, the
words to be emphasized are moved to position 1, the verb
is transformed into a word group introduced by parts of
be, become, and *get,* and the original subject (position 1)
is hooked onto the end of the sentence by means of the
preposition *by* (occasionally, *through*):

1	2	3	4
The reporter	gave	the lady	books.

1	2	3	
The lady	*was* given	books *by the reporter.*	

1	2	3	
Books	*were* given	the lady *by the reporter.*	

Notice, however, that the use of this device is greatly
restricted by the kinds of expressions found in the complements:

a. When either complement can be put into the passive
construction, the inner complement is an *indirect object,*
the outer complement is a *direct object.*

b. When only the inner complement can be put into
the passive construction, the inner complement is a *direct object,* the outer complement an *objective complement.*

c. When only a single complement occurs, it is a *direct
object* if it can be put into the passive construction, a

subjective complement (predicate complement, attributive complement) if it cannot.

For a native speaker of English, these restrictions are of minor importance. His sense of the language is sufficient to guide him. For the grammarian, however, who can be seriously troubled by such so-called idioms as *She looked daggers*(.) or *We talked dogs*(.), the use of the passive construction as a test of the kinds of complements present in the standard 1, 2, 3, 4 construction is of major importance.

4.11   The inner complement (position 3) is remarkable in that it can be *de*-emphasized as well as emphasized. To accomplish this result, it is transformed into a prepositional word-group by the addition of *to* or *for:*

	1	2	3	4
	The reporter	gave	the lady	books.

	1	2	3
	The reporter	gave	books *to the lady*.

	1	2
	Books	were given *to the lady* by the reporter.

In the first example, the group *the lady* is a *must* element of the sentence; in the other examples, it has been demoted in function to the role of a movable modifier by the introduction of the preposition *to:*

	1	2	3
	The reporter	gave	books *to the lady*.

	1	2	3
To the lady,	the reporter	gave	books.

It should be noticed that *to the lady* is neither more elegant nor more explicit in these constructions than *the lady* in the other construction:

	1	2	3	4
	The reporter	gave	*the lady*	books.

It is simply a different type of word-group (prepositional versus noun) which relegates *the lady* to a secondary role among the constituents of the sentence.

4.12 Like the fixed 1, 2, 3, 4 order of the standard English sentence, the fixed order of modification tends to limit emphatic variation. Yet even here, especially in writing of a frankly literary quality, English is by no means lacking in resources. The language possesses a number of fossil constructions, chiefly drawn from medieval and legal French, in which single word modifiers occurring *after* the word they modify carry the principal stress of the word-group:

$$\overset{s}{\text{heirs } male}$$

$$\text{the body } \overset{s}{politic}$$

$$\text{God } \overset{s}{Almighty}$$

$$\text{devil } \overset{s}{incarnate}$$

$$\text{chapter } \overset{s}{ten}$$

Similarly:

$$\text{Edward the } \overset{s}{First}$$

$$\text{John the } \overset{s}{Baptist}$$

$$\text{William the } \overset{s}{Conqueror}$$

$$\text{St. John the } \overset{s}{Martyr}$$

By analogy with these, we can reverse many other modifiers to bring them under the principal stress and hence make them emphatic:

$$\text{soldiers } \overset{s}{three}$$

$$\text{water } \overset{s}{enough}$$

the day *following*^s

the journey *inland*^s

A skillful writer can make use of such reversed modifiers to great stylistic advantage, particularly when he places them under emphatic stress:

The clown *absolute*^s differs from the actor *droll*^s.

In estimating the emphatic effects of reversal, however, we should not forget that certain modifiers invariably follow the word that they modify. These include (1) the space pointing words *here* and *there* (Fig. 9); (2) two- and three-syllable words normally used as adverbs and space-prepositions (*after, before, behind, ahead, around, beneath, between, beyond, under, across, within, underneath,* etc.); and (3) past participle forms:

> this man *here*
> that man *there*
> my brother *alone*
> the ground *beneath*
> the space *within*
> the space *around*
> the money *obtained*
> the song *sung*

4.13 Because overuse spoils their effectiveness, the various devices for securing variations of sentence emphasis should be sparingly and carefully employed. They are not, as teachers often intimate, inherently weaker than the usual constructions. Proper use of the "passive," the *it is, there is* formulae, and the reversed modifiers can be a valuable aid in writing. On the other hand, too frequent use of these devices is to be avoided because it robs them of their emphatic function. Where everything is emphatic, nothing is emphatic.

5 | Connectives

5.1   Some elements in sentences have *practical* meaning; some have only *grammatical* meaning. The
former stand for (i.e., are signs for, are symbolically correlated with) various objects, events, processes, ideas, and
qualities found in the everyday practical world around
us. The latter merely indicate the grammatical relations
of such words; they "stand for" nothing ever found in the
practical world. Thus in the sentence *A reporter call-ed
the lady name-s(.)*, the words *reporter, call, lady,* and
name have practical meaning, while the words *a* and
the and the elements *-ed* and *-s* have only grammatical
or relational meaning. A word having practical meaning
is a *full word*. A word having only grammatical meaning
is an *empty word* (function word, frame word), i.e., a
word empty of practical meaning. The systematic use of
empty words, the third main device of English grammatical structure, is surpassed in importance only by
fixed word order. Essentially, empty words provide a
grammatical framework within which the meanings of
the full words operate.

5.2   Many words never occur with the practical
meaning of a full word. Others may occur in
some contexts as empty words and in some contexts as
full words:

EMPTY WORD: New York¹ *is* ('s)² ruined.

FULL WORD: New York¹ *is*² no more.

EMPTY WORD: New York¹ *has* ('s)² lost its fight for reform.³

FULL WORD: New York¹ *has*² many riches.³

In either case, empty words usually signalize loss of practical meaning in one way or another.

a. When pronounced aloud, they show marked loss of stress, phonetic weakening, or distinct syllabic dependence upon a previous word:

> New York's ruined.
> New York's lost its fight for reform.
> I'll do this.
> I should've done it.

Compare the common student spelling:

> I should *of* done it.

b. They can be usually omitted without material change of sense:

> I am feeling (*pretty*) tired.
> (*The*) boy meets (*a*) girl.

c. When literally interpreted, they make nonsense:

> I am feeling *pretty* tired.
> I feel *awfully* good.

5.3 English empty words were originally full words which have lost practical meaning because of constant repetition in certain kinds of contexts. For instance, *very* once meant "truly," *rather* meant "earlier," *of* is an altered form of *off*, *for* is an altered form of *fore,* and *than* is an altered form of *then.* The process of development into empty words is easily followed:

> I will do this *rather* ("earlier"), *then* that.
> I would *rather* do this *than* that.
> I would *rather* eat *than* sleep.

> I feel *rather* ill.
> A chip *off* the old block.
> A chip *of* the old block.

In spoken English, this process still goes on:

> He was *dead.*
> He was *dead* tired.
> He was *dead* right.

> Each spring I *got* a cold.
> I wrote when I *got* settled.
> Then he *got* writing her every day.

5.4   Detailed discussion of the fifteen classes of English empty words is unnecessary here. It is enough to realize that they are all concerned with setting up a relational connection between something before and after them or with expressing one's feelings about what one is stating. Thus there are two main types: (1) *connecting words* (including conjunctions, prepositions, pronouns, etc.); and (2) *tone words* (including articles, intensifiers, auxiliaries, etc.). For native speakers of English trying to write the language, the following types need particular attention:

a. The connecting words used in prepositional word-groups: *prepositions* (hooking words)

b. The connecting words used with subject-predicate word-groups: *conjunctions* (linking words)

c. The tone words used in verb word-groups: *auxiliaries* (helpers)

It will help us to remember that while the total number of full words is enormous, the number of empty words is relatively limited.

5.5 **Prepositions** (hooking words) are empty words used to hook nouns, pronouns, and word-groups onto preceding words, word-groups, and sentences:

> books
> > *of*
> > > poems
> the thought
> > > *of*
> > > > her
> I relieved him
> > > *of*
> > > > his well-filled purse.
> There is truth
> > > *in*
> > > > what you say.

Their function is the *secondary* modification of preceding elements, accomplished by relating to them things, persons, processes, ideas, and qualities additional to those referred to in the fixed structural elements of the sentence:

1	2	3	4
The reporter	gave	the lady	books.

1	2	3
The reporter	gave	a lady

> on   from
> > *The News*   *Duluth*

> 4
> books   in
> > of   that *garden.*
> > > *Italian poems*

Here *The News, Duluth, Italian poems,* and *garden* are subordinate terms brought into the scope of the sentence by means of the prepositions *on, from, of,* and *in.* In form, prepositions often resemble directives and conjunctions. From directives they can be distinguished by position, function, and lower stress, and from conjunctions by the fact that they select "objective" and "possessive" forms of the following pronouns:

> of *her*
> of *them*
> by *him*
> of *his*

Yet by the continuous transference and truncation of English constructions, directives, conjunctions, and modifiers (*like, unlike, near,* etc.), are constantly being converted into prepositions:

> folks
> *back*
> home.
> I am taller *than* he is.
> I am taller *than* he.
> I am taller
> *than*
> him.

Some of these conversions (notably that of *than*) are still unacknowledged in formal written English.

5.6 Nine one-syllable prepositions (*at, by, for, from, in, of, on, to,* and *with*) form the basis of the English prepositional system. According to the *New English Dictionary,* these have an alleged variety of meanings, ranging from sixty-three (for *of*) to some fifteen (for *for*). The meanings, however, are not expressed by the prepositions themselves but are inferred from the surrounding contexts. The primary grammatical relations expressed by our fourteen one-syllable prepositions are actually very few:

a. The relation of location: *at* ⊂○

                         by ○○○

                         in ◎

                         on ⦸

b. The relation of direction: *to* → ○

                         from ○ →

                         up ↑

                         down ↓

                         off ○↗

                         through ⊖→

                         out ○→→

c. The relation of association: [1]

                         of (originally off) ←

                         for (originally fore) →

                         with (originally a +
                              blend of *mid* with
                              "against, opposed")

All of them have an underlying space significance. Collectively, they may be said to express *case relation* similar to that expressed in such inflected languages as Latin, Greek, Sanskrit, and Georgian by certain case endings of nouns and pronouns. Or, to put the relation in another way, they convert nouns, pronouns, and noun groups into modifiers.

5.7 The basic prepositional system of English is too restricted to indicate all the relations that we may need in writing and speaking. The location of something in respect to something else can involve other possibilities than being "in contact with it" (*at*), "inside it" (*in*), "on top of it" (*on*), and "beside it" (*by*). Something may need to be located in time rather than in space; actions may involve *instruments* and *agents; association*

---

[1] The basic distinction here is between *close association,* as expressed by *of,* and *loose association* as expressed by *for* and *with,* or, to put the matter in another way, between *permanent* versus *transient* association.

between persons and things may be of very varied character. To accommodate these further relations, the basic system of English has been expanded in several directions:

a. The simple prepositions have been *transferred to* express relations other than those to which they originally applied. Contrast *at* and *by* used to express location with *at* and *by* used to express relations of time:

the house *at* the river : my arrival *at* ten o'clock
the house *by* the river : my arrival *by* ten o'clock

b. Certain two-syllable words built up with prefixes or suffixes, and otherwise used in English as modifiers or directives, have been converted into prepositions: *about, above, across, after, against, among, during, inside, around, outside, between, beside(s)*.

c. Certain one-syllable prepositions have been combined to form double prepositions: *into, onto, throughout, until, unto, upon, within, without; down at, down from, down to, in at, in from, off at, off from, up at, up from, up to,* etc.

d. A special class of group prepositions has been created:

(1) From single modifiers or modifying groups followed by simple prepositions: *according to, due to, relating to, prior to, subsequent to,* etc.

(2) From contexts in which one prepositional word group was originally followed by another: *by reason of, by way of, for purposes of, in accord with, in case of, in company with, in connection with, in (the) event of, in line of, in lieu of, in place of, in regard to, in view of, on account of, on behalf of, because of,* etc. Habitual use of these group prepositions in certain recurring contexts has led to loss of stress and loss of practical meaning; they are used almost as if they were single words. Contrast:

The garden lies in the view of your house.
I killed him in view of your decision.

In constructions of this kind, the omission of *the* is a sign that a group preposition has become fully established.

5.8 The result of all this expansion of the basic prepositional system of English has been to create a total system of high complexity. Yet it functions according to rather simple principles:

a. Every simple preposition expresses a relation different from that of all other simple prepositions within the same *locational, directional, associational, agental,* or *time* group.

b. Any transferred preposition contrasts both with all other prepositions in the same relation group and with itself as used in another relation group.

c. The complex, double, and group prepositions subdivide the general grammatical relations expressed by the simple prepositions.

Thus, *by* as used in *by the house* contrasts with *at, in, on, beside,* etc., in the same context: *at the house, in the house, on the house, beside the house.* Again, *by* as used to express location in *by the house* contrasts with *by* as used to express time in *by ten o'clock* or instrument in *killed by a gun.* Further, the simple instrumental relation in *killed by a gun* is enriched and particularized when a group preposition is used: *killed by means of a gun, killed by use of a gun,* etc. What this amounts to is self-evident. The total English prepositional system is governed by a kind of scale of explicitness, whereby the basic relations of *location, direction,* and *association* are progressively subdivided and enriched as transferred simple prepositions, complex prepositions, double prepositions, and group prepositions are brought into the scheme:

SIMPLE	TRANSFERRED SIMPLE	COMPLEX	DOUBLE	GROUP
General relations	More explicit subdivision	Still more explicit subdivision	Still more explicit subdivision	Most explicit subdivision

5.9 Difficulties in the use of prepositions are likely to be due to regional backgrounds and to lack of acquaintance with the conventions of the written language. They can be easily summarized:

a. The word *till* is used in some regional varieties of spoken English to express relations of time and location:

> ten minutes *till* ten
> He went *till* Indianapolis.

Written English usually uses *to* in such cases:

> ten minutes *to* ten
> He went *to* Indianapolis.

b. Written English is said to substitute *until* for *till* in such contexts as the following:

> I cared for my mother *until* ('til) her death.

c. Written English is often said to prefer the group preposition *in addition to* rather than the complex preposition *beside(s)*:

> *In addition to* weapons, I took food.
> *Beside(s)* weapons, I took food.

d. The prepositions *beneath, within, throughout* occur rather frequently in written English, rather infrequently in everyday speech:

> the cellar *beneath* the house
> a room *within* the house
> poverty *throughout* the world

Figure 4

THE SYSTEM OF PREPOSITIONS

RELATION	Simple PRIMARY	TRANSFERRED	Complex	Double	Group
1. Location	at by in on	down from off out through up	aboard, above, across, after, against, amid, before, beneath, beside, between, beyond, near, next, over, past, under	inside, outside, through-out, toward(s), under-neath, upon, within, with-out; down *at, by, in, on;* off *at, by, in, on;* out *at, by, in, on; up at, by, in, on*	in back of in front of inside of on board (of) on either side (of) on top of outside of
2. Direction	down from off out through to up	at by in on	aboard, about, across, after, against, among, around, between, beyond, over, under	inside, outside, toward(s), underneath; *into, onto;* down *to, from;* off *to, from;* out *to, of, from;* up *to, from;* near *to,* next *to;* over *to; to* within, from among	in back of, in front of inside of on top of on board (of) on either side (of) outside of

3. Association	for of with	at in on to	concerning, except, excepting, including, notwithstanding (and various metaphorical uses of the above: *beyond* reproach, *beneath* reproach, *under* suspicion, etc.)	upon, within, of from	according to, by way of, due to, in accordance with, in addition to, in case of, in connection with, in place of, in regard to, in view of, instead of, on account of, on behalf of, owing to, relative to, with respect to
4. Agency		by from through with		out of	by agency of by dint of by means of
5. Time		at, by from of (to) through	after, around, before, between, beyond, during, past, pending, since, until	towards, until, after	

e. Spoken English is extremely rich in double prepositions, many of which are not encountered in the formal written language:

> I took the book *off of* the table.

On the other hand, the written language possesses many group prepositions that are virtually unknown in everyday spoken English. We must conclude that the spoken language tends to use the double preposition, as the written language uses the group preposition, to secure maximum explicitness of relation. Here, then, is a fundamental difference of grammatical device.

f. The group preposition *in regards to* is replaced in written English by *with regard to, in regard to, regarding:*

> I have written *with regard to* your letter.
> I have written *in regard to* your letter.
> I have written *regarding* your letter.

5.10 Significant as these differences seem, they are subsidiary to a wise and controlled use of the entire system of prepositions in English. That involves, first and foremost, a proper understanding of the *scale of explicitness* (5.8). There are many occasions in writing when the relation between the names of two things needs to be expressed only in the most general, least explicit terms; there are others when the relation needs to be analyzed in the greatest detail. Only the writer can judge which he needs. The scale of explicitness has frequently been misused. There are writers constitutionally incapable of employing a simple preposition when a group preposition is available and the overuse of *prior to, subsequent to,* etc., has become a mark of jargon. In legal English, where a significant judgment may depend on the exact relations between words, there may be some excuse for this—the language of the law is written not so much to be understood as not to be misunderstood. In normal written English, excessive use of group prepositions undoubtedly makes for a muddy, colorless style. Just as a sentence in which everything is emphatic is a sentence in which nothing is emphatic, so a sentence in which everything is explicit is one in which nothing is immediately explicit. Both emphasis and explicitness need to contrast with their opposites. The scale of explicitness is a very important device of English grammar which will reappear as we examine the conjunctions and the verbal helpers. All of its potentialities should be used by the writer.

5.11 Conjunctions (linking words) are connective empty words used to link words or word-groups in non-case relationships (see 5.6, 5.14–5.17, 9.8). They may be distinguished from other classes of empty words as being the only class used to establish direct connection between subject-predicate word-groups:

> The girl was pretty *and* I liked her.
> The girl was pretty *so* I liked her.
> I liked the girl *for* she was pretty.
> I liked the girl *because* she was pretty.

Many conjunctions may be distinguished from prepositions in similar contexts by the fact that they require no change of form of following pronouns (5.5): contrast *the egg and I* with *the sight of her.*

5.12 The use of conjunctions is governed by a *scale of explicitness* similar to that of prepositions. Thus the situation expressed in the examples above can be most simply stated *The girl was pretty; I liked her*(.) It suggests an additive connection between the two groups but does nothing further to analyze the details of this connection. In *The girl was pretty so I liked her*(.), *I liked the girl for she was pretty*(.), and *I liked the girl **because** she was pretty*(.), the nature of the connection is made clear; *so, for,* and *because* all explicitly reveal it as some kind of reason-result relation. What, therefore, is unstated but potential in *The girl was pretty; I liked her*(.) and in *The girl was pretty **and** I liked her*(.) is stated unequivocally in *I liked the girl **because** she was pretty*. All these examples refer to the same basic situation. They differ in the degree of explicitness with which the two subject-predicate groups are linked together.

5.13 Like the basic prepositions, the basic conjunctions—whatever their ultimate origin—are now one-syllable empty words: *and, as, but, if, or, nor; so, for; then, than, thence, that, though; what, when, whence, where, which, who, why, how*. Like the simple (i.e., one-syllable) prepositions, they easily fall into definite relational classes.

5.14 *Coupling conjunctions* establish mathematical relations between all kinds of word-groups and also between single words: *and* (addition, +), *but, yet* (subtraction, −), *as, than* (comparison, =), *or, nor* (alternation, ∼).

> The girl was pretty *and* I liked her.
> to have wealth *and* to hold it
> shadow *and* substance
> The girl was homely *but* I liked her.
> poor *but* attractive
> poor *as* a church mouse
> I sang *as* I felt.
> love greater *than* life
> taller *than* a lamp post
> A mink *or* an otter was lurking there.
> She was not pretty *nor* did I like her.

5.15 *Illative conjunctions* (*for* and *so*) establish a relation of illation or logical inference between subject-predicate groups only; they never connect single words or other types of word-groups. When *so* is used, the reason for a consequence is before it:

> The girl was pretty *so* (→) I liked her.

When *for* is used, the reason for a consequence follows it:

> I liked the girl *for* (←) she was pretty.

5.16 *Qualifying conjunctions* (*if, since, though, while, because, although,* etc.) convert one subject-predicate group into a movable modifier (*qualifier,* see 4.7) of another:

> The girl was liked *since* she was pretty.
> *Since* she was pretty, the girl was liked.
> The girl, *since* she was pretty, was liked.

These conjunctions, the only ones permitting free movement of the word-group after them, are occasionally used to connect single words to subject-predicate groups:

> The girl was poor *if* pretty.
> The girl, *if* pretty, was poor.
> *If* pretty, the girl was also poor.

5.17 *Incorporating conjunctions* (*what, who(m), which, when, whence, where, whether, whither, why, how, that*) incorporate one subject-predicate or verbal group into another subject-predicate group as subject, complement, or group modifier:

> 1
> *Where I had been* was none of his business.
> 1 2 3

> 1 2 3
> I didn't know *what to do.*

> 1
> The reasons *why I asked* must have been obvious.
> 2 3

> 1 2 3
> *How he got there* is unknown.

All incorporating conjunctions except *that* and the transferred *if* occur otherwise as question words (interrogatives) and have become conjunctions by conversion of this original function:

> *How* did this happen?
> He asked me *how it happened.*

> *Where* is the fire?
> He asked me *where the fire was.*
>
> *Who* was there?
> He told me *who was there.*

This class of conjunctions also functions as a class of *substitute words* (8.3–8.6) referring to some word or situation before or after. *That* (→) is unique in that its referent (*postcedent*) follows it:

> I told him *that he was a sick man.*

All the others refer to something in a preceding context (*antecedent* ←):

> The place *where I went* is no other man's concern.

This distinction is signaled by the initial *th-* of *that* as contrasted with the initial *wh-* (originally *hw-*) with which all the others at one time commenced (Fig. 9).

5.18 The relations of connection expressed by the simple conjunctions thus form the following rather simple scheme:

RELATION	SYMBOL
1. Addition: *and*	+
2. Subtraction: *but, yet*	−
3. Comparison: *as, than*	=
4. Alternation: *or, nor*	~
5. Illation: *for, so*	← →
6. Qualification: *if, since, though, while, because, although*	≡
7. Incorporation: *that; what, who(m), which, when, whence, why, how*	← ; →

As can be readily seen here, classes 6 and 7 are "subordinating" conjunctions, all the others being "coordinating." This, then, is the primary conjunctional system of English.

5.19   The simple conjunctions of the primary system
are too few to express all the relations of connection between words and word-groups that might need
expression. Like the simple system of prepositions, this
system has been greatly expanded:

a. The simple conjunctions are used to express relations other than those which they originally expressed.
These may be called *transferred* conjunctions. Contrast
while as a *qualifying* with *while* as an *alternative* conjunction, and *when* as an *incorporating* with *when* as a
qualifying conjunction:

> He made no remarks *while* he was here.
> He could do this *while* he could not do that.
> He asked me *when* he should come.
> He made no such remarks *when* he was present.
> He would make some remarks *if* he were here.
> I asked him *if* he had been there.

b. Simple conjunctions are built up into *double conjunctions,* many of which are also freely transferred to
express other relations than those which they originally
expressed: *however, such as, whatever, whenever,
wherever, whichever, whoever, whosoever, why ever,
although, whereas,* etc.

c. Various words containing prefixes and suffixes (i.e.,
derivative words) function in the system as *complex* conjunctions: *after, because, before, lest, provided, provid-
ing, supposing, unless, whether,* etc.:

> *Provided* you come, the arrangement will stand.
> The arrangement will be broken *unless* you come.

Most of these enrich the expression of qualification.

d. English has long possessed certain *paired* (correla-
tive) conjunctions: *as . . . as, either . . . or, neither
. . . nor, rather . . . than.* To these it has added many
others: *as . . . so; although . . . yet, still; while . . .
yet, still; if . . . yet, still, then; when . . . then; not*

only . . . but also; where . . . there, etc. Most of these now express qualification.

e. To expand the expression of qualification and incorporation, various group conjunctions have developed: *as far as, as long as, as nearly as, as closely as, inasmuch as, insofar as, as to how, as to what, as to when, as to where, as to which, as to whom, as to why,* etc.

> I could not object *inasmuch as* he came.
> *Insofar as* he was able, he completed his task.

5.20 The result of all this expansion of the basic conjunctional system has been to build up the expression of qualification and incorporation to a high degree of efficiency. Within the scope of the conjunctions proper, addition, contrast, alternation, and illation have a much less varied expression. To overcome this relative deficiency, recent English has made increasing use of what might be called *transitional adverbs* (conjunctive adverbs) and of word-groups resembling these. They are not conjunctions despite their similarity of function. They differ from conjunctions in these respects: (1) in speech they carry stress; (2) they can be used to introduce dissociated sentences and even paragraphs; (3) they can be moved into the interior of the word-groups which they link; (4) when used to link subject-predicate groups, they are invariably preceded by the final h–l tone-pause pattern (and hence *must* be preceded by the semicolon). The main purpose of the transitional adverbs is to bring to the expression of addition, contrast, alternation, and illation the same final explicitness which is given to qualification and incorporation by the complex, compound, paired, and group conjunctions:

a. Relation of addition: *also, furthermore, moreover, in addition*

b. Relation of contrast: *however, nevertheless, on the one hand, on the other hand*

c. Relation of alternation: *else, otherwise*

d. Relation of illation: *consequently, hence, thus, therefore, for this reason, as a result, for the reason that, in consequence*

The girl is pretty; *moreover,* I like her.
That the girl was pretty was obvious. *Otherwise,* I should not have liked her.

The increasing use of *and, but, yet,* etc., to introduce disconnected sentences is by analogy with the similar use of the transitional adverbs.

5.21 Despite its apparent complexity, the total conjunctional system of English functions according to simple principles remarkably like those which govern the prepositional system:

a. Every conjunction contrasts with all other conjunctions.

b. Any transferred conjunction contrasts both with all other conjunctions in the same relational group and with itself as used in other relational groups.

c. The transferred, complex, compound, paired, and group conjunctions, together with the transitional adverbs, progressively emphasize and make more explicit the connections expressed by the simple primary conjunctions.

SIMPLE CONJUNCTIONS	COMPLEX AND COMPOUND CONJUNCTIONS	GROUP AND PAIRED CONJUNCTIONS AND TRANSITIONAL ADVERBS
Express general relations	More explicit expression of these relations	Most explicit expression of these relations

Figure 5

THE SYSTEM OF CONJUNCTIONS

RELATION	*Simple* PRIMARY	TRANSFERRED	Complex	Double	Paired	Group
1. Addition	and			also furthermore moreover	both . . . and what with . . . and	and also and in addition in addition
2. Contrast	but yet	while though if		however nevertheless	but . . . that except . . . that not only . . . but	on the other hand
3. Comparison	as			such as	as . . . as; as . . . so	
4. Alternation	nor or than		else	or else other than otherwise	either . . . or neither . . . nor rather . . . than whether . . . or	

5. Illation	for so	as when where	consequently hence	and so so that therefore	as . . . so	as a result for the reason that in consequence
6. Qualification	if though while	if	after because before provided providing since supposing unless until	although for all (that) however in that so that whatever whenever wherever whichever whoever	although . . . still although . . . yet if . . . still if . . . then if . . . yet when . . . then where . . . there while . . . still while . . . yet	as closely as as far as as long as as nearly as as soon as inasmuch as in order that insofar as
7. Incorporation	how that what when where which who why		whence whether whither	whatever		as to how as to what as to when as to where as to which as to whom as to why

5.22 So sharply does the conjunctional system of formal written English diverge from that of colloquial spoken English that one must suspect a primary grammatical difference between them. It is true that both systems have the same simple conjunctions. The point is that everyday spoken English has little else. It overworks them shamelessly, transferring them from one relation to another with complete abandon. *Nor, yet, although, provided,* and *until* are almost never found in it; the group conjunctions and the transitional adverbs scarcely ever occur in it. Whatever the merits of its prepositional system, the conjunctional system of colloquial spoken English can only be described as impoverished.

5.23 It is easy to see why. In speech, variations of tone, voice quality, facial expression, and hand movement may tell much about connection of idea with idea. In writing, none of these can operate. Instead, we have to learn to substitute standardized grammatical equivalents for them, and to use those equivalents with the delicate discriminations which, through long years of practice, we have learned to apply automatically in speech. To learn to employ the total conjunctional system accurately and sensibly is to make the most drastic kind of changeover from one habit of language to another.

5.24 To accomplish this changeover, one is usually advised to "use less coordination and more subordination," that is, to use fewer *and's* and *but's,* more *because's, since's,* and *if's,* to substitute qualifying and illative for additive and subtractive conjunctions. This advice should be taken with the proverbial grain of salt. After all, the simplest and most convenient way of linking subject-predicate groups is by means of the semicolon:

The girl is pretty; I like her.

For the most part, this is all we need. Yet—and here is the essential point—when connection between subject-predicate groups *must* be made explicit, it cannot be made explicit by the use of the additive *and* the subtractive *but*. A writer must learn to be reticent; he must ask himself whether the semicolon will not fulfill all requirements of clarity in a given sentence. He must also learn to be expansive, to ask himself whether an illative, qualifying, or incorporating conjunction, or a complex, compound, or group conjunction might not give him greater clarity than the *but* or *and* he might first be tempted to use. Most of all, he must ask himself whether he needs all the subject-predicate groups he is attempting to link by conjunctions. In relatively informal written English, complexity is given to sentences chiefly by verbal, modifier, and noun word-groups, all rather loosely attached, without conjunctions.

5.25   Other practical expedients may be helpful. One may deliberately experiment with the transitional adverbs and non-simple conjunctions. One may isolate simple conjunctions overworked in speech and question their use whenever they suggest themselves. Even to banish them for a while from one's written vocabulary is not too extreme an idea. No writer was ever the worse for temporarily ignoring *and, as, for,* and *so,* as sentence linkers.

5.26   *And.* In spoken English, this most overworked of all conjunctions links any afterthought to anything spoken before it:

I am sick, *and* I need support, *and* I have no money.
I will try *and* get you the books.
I couldn't go to Chicago, *and* Father thought he could.

In the first of these, the relation could be expressed explicitly by *because,* non-explicitly by the semicolon:

Because I am sick and have no money, I need support.
I am sick; I have no money; I need support.

In the second, formal writing would prefer the use of *to:*

> I will try *to* get you the books.

In the third, the submerged contrastive relation should either be left non-explicit or should be explicitly stated by the use of *but, however,* etc.

I couldn't go to Chicago; Father thought he could.
I couldn't go to Chicago, *but* Father thought he could.
I couldn't go to Chicago; Father, *though,* thought he could.

Note, however, that these suggestions for replacing *and* apply only to its use between subject-predicate constructions. As a single word linker it is extremely valuable and should seldom be replaced by *also, as well as, in addition to,* for the sake of mere variety. Otherwise, we might perpetrate the following:

For breakfast, we had ham and eggs, toast, (*also, as well as, in addition to*) coffee.

As. Spoken English uses *as* as a coverall for any kind of qualifying illative, alternative, or incorporating relation:

> He has not been here *as* I know.
> I need your help *as* I am ill.
> I don't know *as* this is the truth.

In written English they would be accurately analyzed:

> He has not been here *as far as* I know.
> *Since* I am ill, I need your help.
> I don't know *if* this is the truth.

Or, alternatively:

> I doubt *if* he has been here.
> I am ill; I need your help.
> I don't know *whether* this is the truth.

For. Unlike *and* and *as, for* is more often abused in written English than in spoken English. Overuse of it marks the unskilled writer; skilled writers tend to replace it with *because, for the reason that, inasmuch as,* etc., or with the semicolon:

We work in the mines *for* we have no other means of support.

We work in the mines *because* we have no other means of support.

We work in the mines; we have no other means of support.

So. As *for* is overused in writing, so the illative conjunction *so* is overused in speech. It contrasts with *for* chiefly in expressing the consequence of a *cause.* Written English tends to replace it as it replaces *for:*

I am too ill for work *so* I am asking you for help.

I am too ill to work; I am asking you for help.

Because I am too ill to work, I am asking you for help.

5.27 The conclusion suggested by these examples is this: the most useful link between the subject-predicate word-groups is not a conjunction at all; it is merely the semicolon, a symbolical substitute for the final declarative tone-pause pattern (h–l) of English (10.3–10.4). In mastering the conjunctional devices, the first step is to learn to make frequent use of the semicolon; the second is to replace *and, as, for, so* whenever explicitness of connection is needed. The rest is practice.

6 : The verb and its helpers

6.1 The system of the English verb is rightly considered to be the most complex grammatical structure in our language. Yet, compared with verbs in Latin, Greek, and Sanskrit, or, for that matter, with those in French and German, plain English verbs possess very few distinctive parts. Once we realize that the past participle forms (*cast, rolled, given, sung, gone,* etc.) are forms conveying the same grammatical information, it will be easy to see from the scheme below that the *bases,* s-parts ("third person singulars"), *past participles,* and *present participles* (*ing*-parts) constitute the relatively few *principal parts* of which the entire verb system is constituted (see Fig. 6).

6.2 In contrast to the simplicity of the system of verbal parts, the total verb system of English is extraordinarily complex—a cubal system rather than

---

Figure 6   *3-part verbs*

BASE	cast
S-PART (3RD SING.)	cast-s
PAST TENSE	cast
PAST PARTICIPLE	cast
PRESENT PARTICIPLE	cast-ing

---

the simple binary system represented by the prepositions and conjunctions. This fact is due to an important grammatical feature of the language: that the verb position in the language (fixed word-order position 2) can be filled not only by the simple verb but also by a headed word-group (verb group). In such a verb group, a head consisting of a base, modified base, replaced base, or amplified base (2.6) of a full verb is preceded by one, or two, or a series of empty words. These, whatever their precise nature, are the verbal auxiliaries (verbal helpers) of English, *the empty words used in verb word-groups:*

1	2	3	4
The reporter	*was **giving***	a lady	books.

1	2	3	4
The reporter	*had been **giving***	a lady	books.

1	2	3
The reporter	*had been about to be **giving***	a lady

4
books.

Whatever their functions, these words preceding the verb head constitute special kinds of modifiers, but being empty words, not full words, they modify the head only grammatically. Their main function is to limit the functions of the verb according to the attitudes and feelings of speakers towards the happenings they may be reporting. When a simple verb is used it merely *times* a happening as past or non-past (i.e., not dissociated from the present time):

	4-part verbs			*5-part verbs*		*8-part verb*
roll	come	seek	go	speak	sing	be (am)
roll-s	come-s	seek-s	go-es	speak-s	sing-s	i-s/are
roll-ed	came	sought	went	spoke	sang	was/were
roll-ed	come	sought	gone	spoke-n	sung	be-en
roll-ing	com-ing	seek-ing	go-ing	speak-ing	sing-ing	be-ing

	1	2	3	4
The reporter	*gave*	the lady	books.

	1	2	3	4
The reporter	*gives*	the lady	books.

When a verb word-group is used, it indicates the particular manner in which a happening is, was, will be, or may be realized:

1   2   3   4

The reporter   *had been giving*   the lady   books.

1   2   3

The reporter   *had been about to give*   the lady

4

books.

1   2   3

The reporter   *might have been giving*   the lady

4

books.

In the simple verb forms of English, all this is left implicit, unanalyzed, unstated; in the verb word-group, it is explicit, analyzed, stated. Since several grammatical relations interlock here in such groups, we had best examine them first.

6.3 **Tense** times a happening with reference to the time of talking or writing about it. If the two times coincide—that is, if something is happening while we are talking or writing—we have *present tense*. If the happening occurred before it is talked or written about, we have *past tense*. If we talk or write about something that has not happened but will happen, we have *future* or *potential tense*. The English simple tenses, i.e., tenses expressed by simple verbal forms, are *past* and *non-past*. The latter does not indicate present time as such but merely times a happening as not being dissociated from the present:

Tomorrow I go to Indianapolis.
Few persons *remember* how they learned to read.
Trees *are* always with us.

In verb word-groups, another kind of tense distinction occurs, that between the *immediate* and the *proximate* (i.e., less immediate). Thus *could* is the proximate of *can, would* of *will, might* of *may; had had* and *had been* are the proximate of *has had, has been.* Similarly, *going* (*to*) expresses the proximate of *about* (*to*):

I am *going to go* to Boston (sometime in the future).
I am *about to go* to Boston (immediately).
I *may go* to Boston. (There is some possibility I may go.)
I *might* go to Boston. (There is less possibility I may go.)

The contrast of immediate and proximate tense is highly significant in English verb word-groups.

6.4 **Mood** (or **mode**) establishes the speaker's or writer's mood about the actuality of a happening. The indicative mood indicates that what he says must be regarded as fact, i.e., as having occurred or as occurring; the so-called subjunctive mood implies that he is doubtful or uncertain about its occurrence:

John's health *is* really bad; he ought to quit work.
If John's health *be* really bad, he ought to quit work.

Although the subjunctive is gradually dying out of the language, English is rich in devices for expressing one's psychological moods toward happenings that are imaginary. We can, for instance, clearly indicate whether a non-actual (i.e., unrealized) happening can be regarded as an intention, probability, possibility, necessity, hope, and so forth.

Tomorrow, I *will* go to Boston.
Tomorrow, I *may* go to Boston.
Tomorrow, I *might* go to Boston.
Tomorrow, I *can* go to Boston.
Tomorrow, I *must* go to Boston.
Tomorrow, I *should* go to Boston.

Our apparatus for expressing mood suggests that in the use of verb word-groups, the speaker's or writer's mental attitudes are of great importance.

6.5 Aspect resembles mood in that it expresses the speaker's or writer's attitude toward a happening. In aspect, however, he is primarily concerned with its completion or lack of completion—in short, with the progression of the happening. Mentally, he walks round it and observes it from this angle or that, considering whether it is still proceeding (*imperfect aspect*), completed (*perfect aspect*), beginning (*inceptive aspect*), or happening several times (*iterative* or *repetitive aspect*). In English, the primary distinction seems to be between the imperfect and perfect aspects—a distinction for which we have a well-developed apparatus of expression. Our other aspects are less well-marked grammatically and may be considered aspect-like variants of these two, the iterative and inceptive being variants of the imperfect. Simple verb forms and verb word-groups ending in the verb base do not reveal aspect, or, to put the matter in another way, belong to an *indefinite aspect*. Since the distinction between aspect and tense is somewhat difficult to explain, a fanciful analogy may be helpful to us: in tense, the happening flows past a fixed observer; in aspect, the observer moves round the happening. It is worth remarking that since aspect is the last thing signaled by a verb word-group it is the latest and most important characteristic of the verb left in our minds.

6.6 Voice, which theoretically indicates whether the subject acts (*active voice*), is acted on (*passive voice*), performs the action for itself (*dynamic voice*), or acts on itself (*reflexive voice*), is relatively unimportant in English. Our so-called passive voice is best regarded as a word-order device for giving emphasis to what would normally be inner and outer complements (4.10).

6.7   Verb groups express the aspects of a happening
         by varying the verb part used as the head. Thus
an *ing*-part (present participle) marks a continuing or
imperfect happening (imperfect aspect), a past participle
marks a completed or perfect happening (perfect aspect),
and a simple base marks a happening as neither of these
(indefinite aspect):

| 1 | 2 | 3 | 4 |
| The reporter | was giv*ing* | a lady | books. |

| 1 | 2 | 3 | 4 |
| The reporter | had giv*en* | a lady | books. |

| 1 | 2 | 3 | 4 |
| The reporter | might *give* | a lady | books. |

The role of the verbal helpers is to differentiate these
general aspects even further by marking their detailed
time settings (*tenses*) and special conditions of possible
occurrence (*moods*). Classification of the verbal helpers
depends partly upon their form and partly upon their
positions as constituents of the verb word-group.

6.8   The first major division consists of those verbal
         helpers which can assume the first position in
the verb group. These have a function somewhat analo-
gous to that of *the* and *a* in such headed word-groups as
the handsome reporter, a handsome reporter, i.e., they
identify the head as to tense or mood just as *the* and *a*
identify a noun in terms of one's previous experience.
There are two subdivisions:

a. **Modals** (mood auxiliaries) are stressless verbs that
can occur immediately before a plain base and lack an
s-part: *can, could, dare, may, might, must, need, shall,
should, will, would.* Their purpose is to signalize non-
actual situations, i.e., happenings that have not taken
place, and may never take place, according to the various
attitudes (moods) held by the person who reports them:
possibility, necessity, obligation, intention, condition,
capability:

1	2	3	4
The reporter	*may give*	the lady	books.

1	2	3	4
The reporter	*could give*	the lady	books.

1	2	3	4
The reporter	*will give*	the lady	books.

1	2	3	4
The reporter	*must give*	the lady	books.

The lack of *s*-parts coincides with a similar lack, with the same grammatical significance of *non-actuality,* in the rare subjunctive (hypothetical) forms of simple verbs:

> If he *be* present, our worry is over.
> If he *finish* the work, all will be well.

b. **Timers** are verbs that possess *s*-parts but cannot occur immediately before a simple base used as the head. Here certainly belong the parts of *be* and *have.* Those of *get* and *keep,* which, when combined with appropriate head words, express both tense and minor aspects of the verb word-group, are in the process of becoming verbal helpers:

PAST TENSE; IMPERFECT ASPECT

1	2	3	4
A reporter	*was* giv*ing*	the lady	books.

PAST TENSE; PERFECT ASPECT

1	2	3	4
A reporter	*has* giv*en*	the lady	books.

PAST TENSE; ITERATIVE IMPERFECT ASPECT

1	2	3	4
The reporter	*kept* giv*ing*	the lady	books.

PAST TENSE; INCEPTIVE IMPERFECT ASPECT

1	2	3	4
The reporter	*got* giv*ing*	the lady	books.

Since *be, have, get,* and *keep* can otherwise function as full verbs and possess their own principal parts, they may form constituent initial word-groups within the total verb word-group:

1	2	3	4
The reporter	*has been* giving	the lady	books.

1	2	3	4
The reporter	*has kept* giving	the lady	books.

6.9 The second division of verbal helpers comprises empty words which occur internally in the verb word-group:

1	2	3
The reporter	may *have been about* to give	a lady

4
  books.

The natural point of division between these words and the initial word or words is shown by the possibility of inserting a qualifying adverb between the two:

1	2
The reporter	may *presumably* have been about to give

1	2
The reporter	had been *presumably* about to give

This parallels exactly the structure of noun word-groups, in which a similar word may be inserted immediately after *the* or *a:*

> The *presumably* handsome reporter

We may call all internal verbal helpers *combining helpers,* their purpose being to permit the further interlocking of tense, mood, and aspect.

6.10 The first class of combining helpers comprises *have, had, be, being* and *been* (i.e., principal parts of *be* and *have*). The function of these words is to combine the modals with tense and aspect indications:

1	2	3	4
The reporter	may *be* giving	a lady	books.

1	2	3	4
The reporter	may *have* given	a lady	books.

1   2   3
The reporter   may *have been* giving   a lady
4
books.

The first of these combines the mood of possibility, present tense, and imperfect aspect; the second, the mood of
possibility, past tense, and perfect aspect; the third, the
mood of possibility, past tense, and imperfect aspect. *Be*
and *have been* can be used only before a present participle, i.e., they are always used in the expression of imperfect aspect; *have* alone can be used only before a past
participle, i.e., it is always used to express perfect aspect.
Be marks the non-past tense; *have* and *have been* mark
the past tense.

6.11   The second class of combining helpers consists
of the word *to* either alone or modified by a
preceding *about* or *going*. *To* marks the *potential tense*
of an occurrence; that is to say, it marks it as something
that is not happening and has not happened but is going
to happen. When *about* precedes *to* the potentiality is
immediate; the happening is on the point of starting
(*immediate potential tense*). When *going* precedes *to,* the
potentiality is more remote; some time will elapse before
the happening starts (*proximate potential tense*). Contrast:

1   2   3   4
The reporter   is *to give*   a lady   books.
1   2   3   4
The reporter   is *about to give*   a lady   books.
1   2   3   4
The reporter   is *going to give*   a lady   books.

The potential tense, whether simple or combined with
the perfect or imperfect aspects, may be *retrospective* as
well as *prospective:*

1   2   3   4
The reporter   *was* to give   a lady   books.

```
      1                    2                  3
The reporter      was about to be giving      a lady
      4
   books.

      1                         2                     3
The reporter      was about to have been giving      a lady
      4
   books.
```

When the potential tense is combined with initial *ought,*
has (had) it may express, in addition to potentiality,
obligation and *necessity:*

```
      1                2              3            4
  The reporter      has to give    the lady     books.

      1                2              3            4
  The reporter      ought to give  the lady     books.
```

Finally, either of these, the potential tense, and either of
the two major aspects may be combined into a verb word-
group:

```
        1                        2
  The reporter        ought to have been about

                            3           4
    to have been giving    a lady    the book.
```

6.12 Valid distinctions between written and spoken
English in the use of the verbal helpers are
relatively few. Even those that exist are often subject to
much pro and con argument, i.e., they are questions of
usage rather than of grammar (7.1–7.7).

a. In spoken, and to some extent in written, English, a
qualifier is often inserted between the potential marker
to and the following verb base (2.8, fn. 3):

```
The reporter      has to eventually give      the lady
   books.
```

The use or non-use of this "split infinitive" should be
conditioned by the demands of emphasis and euphony
rather than by any imaginary "grammatical principle."

b. Except in first-person questions, *shall* is seldom used by many literate Americans. A small number of persons, however, make a systematic distinction between *shall* and *will*, a distinction based upon eighteenth-century attempts to rationalize English grammar. According to this, the normal use of *shall* and *will* blends the forms as follows:

SINGULAR	PLURAL
I *shall*	we *shall*
you *will*	you *will*
he, she, it *will*	they *will*

When the mood of determination needs to be expressed, these forms are reversed: I *will*, you *shall*, etc. Although the distinction is a useful one, common sense would dictate that it should be followed only if one feels easy in making it. It is much preferable to reserve *shall* for first-person questions and *will* for all expressions of mood than to indulge in such muddled recollections of the distribution of *shall* and *will:*

He *shall* be in Boston tomorrow.
You *shall* note the distinction between communism and democracy.

c. The modals *should* and *would* can be used to express the same distinctions as *shall* and *will*. Here again, however, most literate Americans tend to use *should* only in first-person questions and to use *would* in all other cases. In addition, *would* often appears both in spoken and written American English to express iterative aspect in the past tense:

When I was young, I *would* go to school.

6.13 All these are relatively slight details. The principal difficulty in using the verbal system is the tendency to exploit its full scope too often. Spoken English possesses a grammar of verb helpers that is much richer than that of written English. The hypothetical man-in-the-street can scarcely open his mouth without endowing his report of a happening with the most elaborate kind of modal and aspectual overtones. Creature of emotion, he seizes upon every grammatical occasion to express emotional reactions; and his principal emotion carrier is the system of verbal helpers. The writer has to learn to be more restrained. After all, simple verb forms can always be substituted for the complex verb groups to express implicitly what the latter, with their vast array of modal and aspectual complexities, express *explicitly*. And since empty words, for all their usefulness, cannot carry practical meaning, any great concentration of them in a sentence means a dilution of its communicative effectiveness. Like the simple prepositions, the simple verb forms represent the norm of written style. Complex verb word-groups should be withheld for the relatively few occasions when they are really needed.

7 | Word forms I

7.1 The fourth major device of English grammar is the use of altered forms of words (2.6):

> The *man see-s.*
> The *men see.*
> *I* hit *him.* (Compare with *It is* ***I****.*)
> *He* hit *me.* (Compare with *He is* ***he****.*)

This device, less essential to grammatical structure than either word order or the use of empty words, makes the changeover from spoken to written English most difficult and most irritating.

7.2 The fact is, every language exhibits a conflict between the principal grammatical devices and the minor devices. By the process known as analogy, patterns accommodating only a few linguistic phenomena and preserved by sheer frequency of occurrence tend to be refashioned to conform to those accommodating many phenomena. "Irregularities" tend to become "regular." This is particularly true of spoken languages. In the written forms of languages, which are inherently traditional and conservative as compared with speech, "irregularities" persist much longer; and in their persistence, they are apt to acquire a social importance that quite exceeds their linguistic importance. Just as a Sulka tie or a

Brooks Brothers' sport coat may put a social stamp on the wearer, so someone's use of a minor grammatical pattern may mark him as belonging to a desirable social class. Many of the word form patterns of English are definitely of this order.

7.3 Millions of Americans use *who* in all contexts; *whom* still maintains a healthy existence in written English and is considered socially preferable to *who,* even in speech, when preceded by a preposition. Except among the socially insecure, *it is me* is almost invariable in speech; in formal writing, *it is I* is still the preferred form. Such examples could be greatly multiplied. Notice that clarity of statement has nothing to do with these matters; one form is as clear as the other. Nor, since effective speakers and writers are violently partisan both for and against certain of these forms, is there any absolute standard of correctness versus incorrectness, of white versus black. The problem here centers on *usage* —that grammatical battlefield where victory constantly wavers between the radical forces of speech and the conservative forces of writing. Our main concern with usage is to make sure that readers do not have to worry about minor grammatical proprieties rather than what is expressed. This means more than blind adherence to "rules" and "standards." It means that our attitudes toward word forms should be informed, intelligent, judicious. It means that, in this respect at least, a style of writing should attract attention neither from itself nor to itself.

7.4 The grammar of word forms has two facets. One has to do with the varying shapes of words, the other with their behavior. The one involves their changes of form, the other the ways in which they *cross-reference* each other within the web of interrelations forming a context. Both facets are important—and troublesome.

7.5 Individual problems of word shape are best solved through the dictionary. In two major areas, however, the differences between spoken and written English are so marked that memorization will pay huge dividends in time and trouble saved. Anyone who will thoroughly memorize the following tables (Figs. 7, 8) will remove very many of the possible conflicts between what he might write and what readers think he ought to write. In learning written English, as in learning a foreign language, some forms must be drilled into the memory; but the drill should be realistic. The forms should be memorized in groups based upon the resemblances of sound or spelling, as suggested in Fig. 7.

7.6 The word forms given in the two preceding tables represent minor patterns of word formation that exist side by side with major patterns. In speech, therefore, these minor patterns are often modified and reshaped, usually in the direction of the major patterns:

a. Most English verbs are *four-part* verbs with a base form (*roll, seek*), an *s*-form (*roll-s, seek-s*), a past tense form (*roll-ed, sought*) and an *ing*-form (*roll-ing, seek-ing*) (see Fig. 6). In speech, verbs with more or fewer parts than four tend to be made to conform with the four-part pattern:

1) Three-part verbs (Fig. 6) tend to acquire new past tense forms: *shedded, splitted, spreaded, cutted,* etc. In the South and Southern Middle West, however, new three-part verbs are constantly being created through a purely phonetic phenomenon: the loss of the *-(e)d* past tense ending after voiceless or voiced stop consonants and after *-n:*

> Today I *work* hard.
> Last week I *work* hard.
> He *shove* me around.
> I *join* the Army last February.

Figure 7

MINOR VERB PATTERNS (See Fig. 6)

A. VERBS WITH INVARIABLE TENSE FORMS (THREE-PART VERBS)

Group 1	*Group 2*	*Group 3*	*Group 4*	*Group 5*	*Group 6*
shed	let	hit	cut	cast	hurt
spread	set	split	put	cost	burst
rid		slit	shut	thrust	

B. VERBS WITH UNEXPECTED FORMS (PAST PARTICIPLES) AFTER *have* AND *have been* (ALL FIVE-PART VERBS EXCEPT GROUP 7)

Group 1	*Group 2*	*Group 3*
began/have begun	drove/have driven	blew/have blown
came/have come	gave/have given	flew/have flown
drank/have drunk	rode/have ridden	threw/have thrown
ran/have run	wrote/have written	drew/have drawn
sang/have sung		
sprang/have sprung		
swam/have swum		

Group 4	*Group 5*	*Group 6*
broke/have broken	bore/have borne	ate/have eaten
forgot/have forgotten	did/have done	fell/have fallen
froze/have frozen	went/have gone	took/have taken
spoke/have spoken	wore/have worn	
	swore/have sworn	
	saw/have seen	

Group 7

brought/have brought
dived (dove)/have dived
drowned/have drowned

C. VERB PAIRS FREQUENTLY CONFUSED

1.	lie	lay	have lain
	lay	laid	have laid
2.	sit	sat	have sat
	set	set	have set
3.	fall	fell	have fallen
	fell	felled	have felled
4.	rise	rose	risen
	raise	raised	have raised

Figure 8

CERTAIN NOUN PLURALS NOT IN THE REGULAR PATTERN OF FORMATION

Singular marking	Modified base	Modified base plus -es	-en plurals	-im plurals	-es plurals	-i plurals	-ae plurals	-a plurals
none	feet geese lice men mice teeth women	beeves lives calves loaves elves sheaves halves shelves knives thieves leaves wives	brethren children oxen	cherubim seraphim teraphim				
-is					analyses axes bases crises ellipses hypotheses oases synopses syntheses			
-ex					apices appendices codices indices matrices			

	alumni bacilli cacti fungi nuclei radii stimuli termini	alumnae antennae formulae nebulae vertebrae	automata criteria phenomena	agenda bacteria data memoranda
-us		-a	-on	-um

You may need to watch for this tendency in speech to make sure that it is not transferred to the *written* form.

2) Five-part verbs (Fig. 6) tend to align themselves with the four-part pattern by dropping either their past tense form or their past participle form (i.e., form after *have been*). Cf. colloquial spoken English *I have sang, I sung, I have swam, I have ate, I have wrote, she is went,* etc.

b. Of the nouns given in Fig. 8, those with singulars ending in *-ex, -us,* and *-a* tend to form alternative plurals with the usual *-(e)s* ending of English nouns: *apexes* beside *apices, codexes* beside *codices, formulas* beside *formulae, terminuses* beside *termini,* etc. Some of the alternative plurals resulting from this desirable tendency have now gained acceptance in written English.

7.7 In estimating the above modifications, you must remember that written English is a conservative dialect of our language, highly resistant to the innovations of speech—a dialect pruned, regulated, and formalized during the late eighteenth and early nineteenth centuries. The business of the writer is to learn that dialect. The tendencies of the spoken language are not blameworthy, or intrinsically "careless," or reflections of inferior intelligence. As a matter of history, those examined in paragraph 7.6 have operated previously on our language and have produced verb forms and noun forms now considered "standard." But usage is often a matter of fashion; and the great majority of the spoken English forms above are, from the standpoint of the written language, unfashionable. Some of them (notably those in 7.6a.2) were once in fashion and have dropped from fashion; others (like those in 7.6.b) may gradually come into fashion. The practical thing is to memorize and use the forms given in Figures 7 and 8 in the knowledge that they are all acceptable in written English, all fashionable, always appropriate.

8 | Word forms II: Substitution

8.1 **Cross-reference,** the linguistic factor which most influences changes in shape of words, involves two interlocking grammatical devices: (1) the alteration of word forms to show connection with or dependence on other words, e.g., *The **day-s** slip away*(.), *The **day** **slip-s** away*(.), *I gave the books **to her***(.); (2) the use of words or word-groups as substitutes for preceding or following elements in a context, e.g., *When I saw **John**, I knew **him** immediately*(.), *It is too bad **she** got away*(.), ***John** runs faster than **I***(.). The first of these devices is known as *selection,* the second as *substitution.* Since substitution functions within the broader framework of selection, it can be examined first.

8.2 Thinking of substitution, you will first think of such *pronouns* as *I, we, you, he, she, it, they.* In contemporary English, however, the grammatical device covers a much broader territory. Nouns, verbs, fixed and movable modifiers, and even word-groups may serve, on occasion, as substitutes for preceding or following constructions *of parallel form or function.* These may be called *parallel substitutes.*

a. Nouns after *than* or *as* substitute for preceding predicates with noun complements:

I *can play tennis* better than *Mary* (can play tennis).

Alicia *dances the tango* as brilliantly as *Jane* (dances the tango).

b. The verb *do* substitutes for preceding predicates:

> I *play tennis* as well as John *does.*
> We *dance* better than they *do.*
> I will *count the coins* if you *do.*

c. Modals and timers substitute for preceding predicates in which they already appear:

I *will play tennis* if you *will* (play tennis).

I *can climb the hill* if you *can* (climb the hill).

I *have known* better *times* than he *has* (known times).

d. Word-groups substitute for preceding predicates containing complements of the same structure:

Science *was my enemy;* poetry, *my friend.*

My words *were my own;* my actions, *my ministers'.*

e. Modifiers substitute for preceding noun word-groups:

> I prefer *fresh milk* to *homogenized* (milk).

f. Nouns plus prepositions substitute for following nouns plus prepositional word-groups:

This indicates their *connection with* or *dependence on European culture.*

g. Verbs and verbals substitute for following verbs and verbals plus complements:

I *heard* but did not *understand the issue.*

I had *heard* but *had not understood the issue.*

To understand is not necessarily *to love* humanity.

These stand for what *precedes* and *follows them.*

These stand for words *preceding* and *following them.*

Needless to say, the use of parallel substitutes such as these has a marked effect on style. They promote both a desirable economy of expression and the rigid *parallel construction* of word-groups and sentences upon which good twentieth-century writing so much depends.

8.3 The parallel substitutes are not primarily *substitute words;* they are words of other classes used occasionally for substitution. Our other English substitutes are definitely substitute words, primarily employed as substitutes and systematically related in form, or meaning, or both. These *systematic substitutes,* as we may call them, are all basically *pointing words* (deictic words). That is, they represent either something in the relation *speaker—hearer—thing spoken of,* or distance of something or someone from the *speaker* or *hearer,* or proximity of something or someone to the *speaker's* attention. In any case, their underlying meanings concern pointing in space. From space-pointing have developed the person-pointing, number-pointing, direction-pointing, manner-pointing functions which characterize their use in modern English. The usefulness of substitute words lies in abstraction from practical meaning; they allow us to identify or select the things, persons, specimens, or quantities present in a language situation without being distracted by physical properties, colors, and the like. More than any other elements in language, systematic substitutes resemble abstract algebraic symbols. At the same time, in details of form, in the grammatical relations they represent, and in fact that they reflect simple features of the immediate linguistic situation, they seem to hark back to the very beginnings of language. On all these counts, they can raise acute grammatical problems.

8.4 For instance, English nouns and most pronouns cannot change form to indicate whether they are subjects or objects or influenced by prepositions. For these grammatical relations, they have no case endings. Yet eight substitute words which cross-reference with them definitely reflect a case system (5.6; 9.8):

NOMINATIVE:

| I | you | we | they | he | she | it | who |

OBJECTIVE:

| me | you | us | them | him | her | it | whom |

POSSESSIVE:

| my | your | our | their | his | her | its | whose |

REFLEXIVE:

| my- | your- | our- | them- | him- | her- | it- | — |
| self | self | selves | selves | self | self | self | |

Anyone can see that there is something systematic here, yet formal resemblances are interrupted by puzzling divergences. Granted that the "possessive" ending -*s(e)* appears in *his, its, whose,* the "objective" -*m* in *them, him, whom,* and the identical vowel in *me, we, he, she,* by what linguistic atom-change does *I* change to *me, she* to *her,* and *we* to *us?* Why are the first three "reflexives," *myself, yourself, ourselves,* plainly formed from the "possessives" *my, your, our,* while the second four, *themselves, himself, herself,* and *itself,* are formed from the "objectives" *them, him, her,* and *it?* Why is the one form *you* used with both singular and plural reference? Why do we need the "objectives" at all? The answers to all these questions lie deeply buried in the recesses of English linguistic history. Small wonder that colloquial spoken English, in the interests of regularity, is constantly tinkering with this system—forming new "reflexives," *theirselves, hisself,* to conform with *myself, yourself,* and *ourselves;* forming a new plural, *you-all, you-ones,* or *youse;* dropping the form *whom* so that *who* may parallel the incorporating conjunctions (5.17). Yet in the irregularities of its system of substitutes, English is not different from many other languages. In them, also, the systems of personal substitutes show striking irregularities, unexpected changes of form, and preservation of unique grammatical distinctions. The English forms *I—me, we—us, you,* and *she,* which are unrelated in form to the rest of our personal substitutes, and which lie outside the systems of substitutes established below, are of this order.

8.5 Curiously enough, where the English systematic substitutes seem to be most primitive, most obviously reflecting space-pointing in connection with the relation of *speaker—hearer—thing spoken of,* their interconnections stand out most clearly. This space-pointing could be accomplished and was probably first accomplished at the very beginnings of language by hand-pointing. Many of our substitutes, particularly those concerned with the identifying and numeration of objects, seem to be *verbalized gestures* which could coincide with simple hand gestures on the part of the speaker. They may show their origin and purpose through the repetition of certain sounds and sound combinations—a symbolistic repetition which has a one-to-one relationship with obvious movements of the hands: *h-ence, th-ence, wh-ence, h-ith-er, th-ith-er, wh-ith-er; eith-er, oth-er, neith-er, ev-er, nev-er, th-is, th-at, th-ese, th-ose, th-ey, th-ere, th-en, th-ence, th-ither, th-us; wh-o, wh-at, wh-ich, wh-ere, wh-ether, wh-en, wh-ence, wh-ither, wh-y; tha-t, wha-t, i-t, augh-t, naugh-t; ea-ch, whi-ch, mu-ch, su-ch; the-re, he-re, whe-re;* and so forth. The chief symbolisms appear to be these:

th-	"pointing there (towards the hearer or thing spoken of)"
h-	"pointing here (towards the speaker)"
wh-	"pointing first here, then there; hence, general indefiniteness, question"

n-	"pointing here and there with a negative gesture; negation"
-er	"pointing both here and here; hence, two, both, dual number"
-t	"pointing there to indicate something less close to the speaker's interest or attention; hence, thing, not person"
-re	"location in space"
-en	"location in time"
-ence	"direction away"

Not all of these symbolisms were originally in the English language. Some which originally were, have become obscured or weakened as the language has developed. Yet, as a whole, the system has reinforced rather than destroyed itself as the centuries of English have passed by. It is as though a deep-seated need for interconnections of form, a definite need for gesture symbolism, has been constantly influencing this area of English grammar. In no other areas do we find systems of form like those shown in Fig. 9.

8.6 If English were not our own language, a rather full (and intrinsically fascinating) treatment of the behavior of substitutes would be needed here. Since it is our own language, it will suffice to make four rather disconnected observations:

a. Systematic substitutes are neither full nor empty words. They resemble *empty words* in that their meaning is purely grammatical, to be defined by the person, gender, number, etc., of expressions for which they substitute. They resemble *full words* in that they ultimately represent practical meaning, though only at second hand. They are best considered as a special class of *substitute words,* coordinate with full words and empty words. The primary word classes of English, therefore, are *full words, empty words, substitute words.*

Figure 9

SOME SYSTEMATIC SUBSTITUTES

CLASS MEANING	POINT MEANING			
	"at that point"	"at this point"	"at this or that point?"	"neither at this nor that point"
1. Relative closeness to speaker's attention: (a) Close, or person (b) Less close, or thing	*this* (*these*) *that* (*those*)	*he she* (AS. *heo*) *it* (AS. *hit*)	*who* (*whom*) *what*	*no one, nobody* *naught, nothing*
2. Number selection: (a) Dual (b) Plural	*they*	(AS. *hie*)	(*whether*) *which*	*neither* *none*
3. Space occurrence	*there*	*here*	*where*	*nowhere*
4. Time occurrence	*then*		*when*	*never*
5. Direction between two places	*thither*	*hither*	*whither*	
6. Direction away from speaker	*thence*	*hence*	*whence*	
7. Extent or manner of occurrence	*thus*	*how*	*why*	*not*

b. The differences between the formal written language and the colloquial spoken language in the use of substitute words are not very marked.

1) Colloquial spoken English often uses *them* as the plural form of *this* and *that;* written English uses *these* and *those:*

> *Them men* had arrived.
> *These* (*those*) men had arrived.

2) Colloquial spoken English often reinforces *this, that,* (and *them*) with *here* and *there* immediately following (4.12):

> *This here* (food) is good.
> *That there* (food) is good.
> *Them there* (sausages) are good.

Written English, where it uses this reinforcement at all, places it *after* a noun.

> *This* book *here* is good.
> *That* book *there* is good.
> *These* books *here* are good.
> *Those* books *there* are good.

3) Colloquial spoken English often splits *you* (singular and plural) into *you* (singular) and *you-all, you-ones, youse* (plural). None of these is so far acceptable in written English, although the original (and necessary) distinction between *thou* and *you* is reflected by them.

4) Colloquial English and folk speech scarcely know the form *whom* at all (7.3). In relatively formal written English it is always used after prepositions, in the most formal English, also under other circumstances (9.19).

c. Most substitute words represent preceding words or constructions (their *antecedents,* i.e., foregoers). *It* and *there,* however, often represent following words or constructions (*postcedents,* i.e., aftergoers):

> *It* is well you *came.*
> *It* is *raining.*
> *There* came *a man into the house.*
> *There* was *a gap in the conversation.*

d. All substitute words capable of changing their word forms (*I, me; we, us; they, them; he, him; she, her; we, us; who, whom*) do so under the influence of the further grammatical device of *selection.*

9 | Word forms III: Selection

9.1 **Selection** is the grammatical device whereby one word or construction can dictate the choice of form in another. Thus, in the first example below, the singular noun *duck* selects the *s*-form (scream-*s*) of the following verb; in the second example, the plural noun *duck-s* selects the base (scream) of the verb; in the third example, the feminine noun *duchess* selects the feminine form (*she*) of the following substitute word; in the fourth, the preposition *to* selects the "objective" form (him) of the following substitute word; in the fifth, the plural noun *duck-s* selects the plural form (*these*) of the preceding numerator:

1. The *duck scream-s.*
2. The *duck-s scream.*
3. The *duchess* smiled as *she* greeted me.
4. *Someone* had given the book *to him.*
5. *These duck-s* had been screaming.

9.2 In modern English, only nouns, noun substitutes (pronouns), verbs, and prepositions can exercise selection; only noun substitutes (pronouns) show its full range. Where it is exercised, it is for the following grammatical purposes:

a. Nouns, and personal substitutes of the third person, reiterate their number forms in following verbs:

> *The duck scream-s.*
> *The duck-s scream.*
> *It scream-s.*
> *They scream.*

b. Nouns anticipate their number forms in the words *a, one, this (these), that (those)*:

> *A duck* is screaming.
> *This duck* is screaming.
> *These duck-s* are screaming.
> *That duck* is screaming.
> *Those duck-s* are screaming.

c. Nouns, and personal substitutes of the third person, reiterate their sex classification (gender) in following pronouns:

> *Jane* was generous; *she* gave me *her* hat.
> Every *man* there immediately took *his* leave.
> Every *girl* there immediately took *her* leave.

d. The personal substitutes (personal pronouns) *I, he, she, it, we, they, you* reiterate their reference to the speaker (*I*), the hearer (*you*), and the thing or person spoken of (*it, he, she, we, they, you*) in forms of the one verb *be:*

> *I am* sick and sorry.
> *You are* sick and sorry.
> *It is* a sorry matter.
> *She is* a sick girl.
> *He is* a sick man.

e. Verbs select case forms of preceding and following substitutes:

> *The troops shot the men.*
> *They shot them.*
> *It was he.*

f. Prepositions select "objective" case forms of the substitutes following them; with the exception that *of* can also select the possessive form:

> Someone gave the book *to him.*
> *In her,* we see the first Christian martyr.
> I read that book *of his.*

In conventional grammar, where a grammatical relation is *reiterated* (a, b, c, d above) there is said to be "concord" or "agreement": the selected form is described as "agreeing" with the selecting word. The other cases (e, f above) are said to be examples of "government": the form after the verb or preposition is described as being "governed" by it.

9.3 Of the four grammatical relations (*number, gender, person and case*) expressed by selection, only the first two are really integral to English structure. Case and person together are expressed only in six personal pronouns and person alone when the one verb *be* is involved. Even if we dispensed with case and person altogether, our sentences would still make perfect grammatical sense:

> I gave *she* the book.
> I gave the book to *she.*
> He told the soldier to kill *I.*
> I *is* here.
> You *is* here.

Indeed, the latter could be adapted to the singular-plural distinction without the necessity of groping for new forms like *you-all, you-ones,* and *youse.*

> You *is* here (singular).
> You *are* here (plural).

Strange as these may seem to be to a native user of English, their meanings are completely clear. That the grammar of selection is quite unstable, especially when it conflicts with more basic grammatical devices or with the logic of real life, should not, therefore, occasion any surprise. To some degree, the instability depends upon the four grammatical relations themselves. None of them is indispensable for accurate communication in any broad linguistic sense. All are subsidiary to the essential grammatical relations expressed by fixed word order.

9.4   Number, in English, is the most important of the non-indispensable grammatical relations. This is true because English nouns have clear-cut number forms, and partly because number is expressed by many verb and substitute forms as well as by nouns. In English, therefore, number is distinctly emphasized by selection:

> *Every one* of the reporters *was* sincere.
> *Neither* John nor Mary *was* really intellectual.
> *Everybody* was asked to take off *his* coat.

At first glance, English possesses only the *singular* and *plural* numbers. Actually, it has four numbers: a *singular, dual, plural,* and *non-distinctive:*

> a *duck*
> a pair of *ducks* (both *ducks;* the larger of the *ducks*)
> these *ducks*
> We sallied out after wild *duck.*

The latter seems to be confined to hunted creatures ("game"), but see 9.15.

9.5   Gender, in its widest sense, is a method of classifying the universe and its cultural interpretations in terms linguistically manageable. Modern English, Armenian, and Persian have found the classifying factor in logical sex distinctions: *masculine* for males, *feminine* for females, *neuter* for neither. Most languages using sex as a classifying factor have *grammatical gender,* in which the sex gender of a noun is determined by its suffix, or article, or by factors not immediately analyzable. Thus, -*us* marks Latin *fluvius* (river) as masculine; *la,* in French *la sentinelle* (the sentinel), marks it as feminine despite the fact that he is a male; *das,* in German *das Weib* (the woman), marks it as neuter even though a woman is obviously feminine. Pronoun reference (*who* versus *which*) shows quite clearly that the main English distinction is between *personal* and *impersonal,* while the use of *it* breaks down even this distinction:

> I knew *it* was Johnson who was coming.
> I knew *it* was Mary who was coming.
> I knew *it* was a bomb coming.

In the English noun, gender distinctions are either unmarked or very unsystematically marked:

duke	duchess
actor	actress
marquis	marquise
chorus-boy	chorine
he-goat	she-goat

9.6 Our present noun gender distinctions are either borrowed from other languages or represent invention. As if this were not enough, English possesses a system of hidden gender distinctions somewhat resembling the grammatical sex gender of many other languages:

Before I boated *him,* the tuna gave me a real fight.
As *she* came around the bend, the train was fine sight.

In this system, larger animals are usually "he," while smaller animals, personified countries or states, nature, automobiles, trains, sailboats, and motorboats are usually "she." In short, power represents the masculine, grace the feminine. In English, gender is, to say the least, a rather shifty grammatical relation.

9.7 **Person** expresses grammatical relation between a speaker, a hearer, and whatever is spoken of. The speaker represents the *first person;* the hearer, the *second person;* whatever is spoken of, the *third person.* In English, relation of person is transmitted chiefly through the system of substitutes. In all English verbs except *be* it is confined to the indications of the *s*-form *(third person singular)*—a suffixed form indicating at one and the same time *third person, singular number, actuality,* and *non-past tense.* Although English nouns normally select the third person forms of verbs, personal names and vocative expressions are often understood as indicating the second person of the verb:

> *Mac,* give me a match!
> *Sailor,* give me a match!

9.8 **Case** is the relation between nouns, pronouns, and modifiers and other nouns, pronouns, or verbs, in the same grammatical construction. Etymologically, the word means "a falling away" and owes its grammatical application to the erroneous Latin conception that all other cases fell away or declined from the nominative. Fifty-four cases have been postulated for certain little-known Asian languages, and North Georgian seems to possess at least twenty-three. In English, nouns possess no distinctive case endings—the work is done by word order and prepositions. We attribute to nouns the primary distinction between the *nominative* and the *objective cases* on analogy with the pronouns which can substitute for them. The so-called *possessive case* is best thought of as a method of transforming a noun into a modifier, yet *this book of his, this purse of Nan's* could conceivably be thought of as genuine possessives. Probably the least inaccurate method of naming the pronominal cases in English would be to call them the *direct* and the *oblique.*

9.9 If we take the six English pronouns *I, he, she, we, they, who,* as representative of all nouns and pronouns, and the verb *be* as representative of all verbs, the principles of selection can be stated as follows:

SELECTIVE PRINCIPLE 1: A subject selects a verb of the same number and person.

SELECTIVE PRINCIPLE 2: An antecedent selects a pronoun of the same number, person, and gender.

SELECTIVE PRINCIPLE 3: A preposition and any verb except *be* selects the "objective" form of a following pronoun.

SELECTIVE PRINCIPLE 4: The verb *be* selects the "nominative" form of a following pronoun.

SELECTIVE PRINCIPLE 5: A noun selects the singular or plural forms of *this, that* according to its own number.

As rule-of-thumb principles, these five are not objectionable. They do not, however, clarify certain sources of confusion, all of which need mention here.

9.10 Confusion 1. A subject composed of a collective noun may be regarded either as a single entity comprising its units or as a mere accumulation of separate units. If it is the first, it selects a singular verb; if it is the second, a plural:

> The family *is* all collected here.
> The family *are* all collected here.
> The American people *speaks.*
> American people *speak.*

9.11 Confusion 2. Compound subjects composed of two nouns or pronouns linked by *and* normally select a plural verb:

Jack and Jill *were* up the hill.

If, however, the subject is regarded as a unity (i.e., if it functions as a kind of compound) it selects a singular verb:

> Bread and butter *is* what I need.
> Pen and paper *was* what I wanted.

On the same principle, many expressions of time, distance, and measure which seem plural select a singular verb:

> Ten minutes *is* too short a time for that.
> Thirty yards *seems* no great distance.
> Three times five *is* fifteen.

9.12 Confusion 3. When a subject is modified by a following word-group, the subject, not the noun in the word-group, selects the number of the verb:

The main army / of the Celts / *was* in the Black Forest.
Sincerity /, rather than caresses, / *was* what she needed.
Indiana /, as well as neighboring states, / *is* educationally
    advanced.

9.13 Confusion 4. Theoretically, the numerical expressions *many a, such a, no, each, every, no one, nobody, everyone, everybody, someone, somebody, either, neither, none,* etc. select singular verbs and singular following pronouns:

Everybody takes his hat to such functions.
Many a man *has* realized his deficiencies just in time.

In formal writing, this principle is rather rigidly followed, although *none* can be followed either by a singular or a plural according to the number implicit in the context. In speech, and increasingly in less formal writing, the subject is often thought of as collective and is consequently followed by plural verbs and pronouns.

9.14 **Confusion 5.** When nouns of different number are linked by the paired alternative conjunctions *neither . . . nor, either . . . or, rather . . . than,* the verb is theoretically selected according to the number of the nearest noun:

Neither I *nor* the Johnsons were responsible.

In practice, the result is so awkward that the entire construction is often changed:

I *was* not responsible, nor *were* the Johnsons.

9.15 **Confusion 6.** Certain nouns ending in *-s* have apparently no plurals. Or, to put the matter in a better way, their number is non-distinctive:

a. Such common words as *means, remains, headquarters,* etc.

b. Such names of sciences as *mathematics, linguistics,* etc.

c. Such names of countries as the *United States, the Philippines,* etc.

d. Such plural book titles as Percy's *Reliques of Ancient English Poetry, The Adventures of Tom Sawyer,* etc.

In the last century, these normally selected a plural verb; nowadays, they normally select a singular:

The news *is* distinctly good.
Mathematics *is* the language of science.
Percy's *Reliques was* first published in 1785.

9.16 **Confusion 7.** In many types of spoken English, the number distinction between *was/were* and *doesn't/don't* tends to be leveled out in favor of invariable *was* and *don't*. In both instances, the number situation is unique: in *was/were* because the form *were* is our only distinctive past plural verb form; in *doesn't* because an *s*-part with an unusual phonetic modification of the vowel can be readily assimilated to the following *n*. Written English does not make use of the leveled forms.

9.17 Confusion 8. The use of *one* as a genderless pronoun corresponding to French *on* and to German *man* has never been universally popular in spoken and written English. Many sensitive writers replace it by *we, you,* or *they:*

> From this, *we* can realize the futility of lying.
> First *you* turn on the furnace; then *you* light it.
> *They* will have sad hearts this morning in Boston.

In spoken English, it is frequently avoided through the use of *a person, a fellow*—two forms not recommended for use in written English:

> *A person* just cannot tell what to do.
> *A fellow* has to do the best he can.

When *one* is used, it should be cross-referenced, being genderless, to *he* and *his* considered as being also genderless:

One cannot help *his* birth whatever *he* may think of it.
If *one* perceived anything under anesthesia, would *he* forget it on coming to *his* senses?

Otherwise, one of the clumsiest constructions in contemporary writing may result:

One cannot help *his* or *her* birth whatever *he* or *she* may think of it.

9.18 Confusion 9. After parts of the unique verb *be,* the "nominative" forms *I, she, he, we, they,* and *who* are customarily selected in formal writing:

It is *I*.
It was *she* who was to blame.
The guilty persons are *they*.

Since, however, the "objective" forms *me, her, him, us,* and *them* occur after every other verb in the language, the pressure of the total pattern upon this one exceptional case is so powerful that the particular is beginning to conform to the general. In speech, the use of the nominative forms of pronouns after parts of *be* has come to be regarded as characteristic of purists, teachers, professional grammarians, and the socially insecure. Authors of recent fiction tend to avoid the "nominative" forms even in writing.

9.19   Confusion 10. The *who/whom* confusion is a major bugbear of contemporary English usage. Most speakers do not possess the form *whom* at all; with them, *who* is invariable. Careful speakers and most good writers follow a definite principle: they use *whom* immediately after a preposition, and *who* in all other cases. Some few of us still use *who* and *whom* according to the strictest dictates of the conventional grammar book, i.e., we write *whom* whenever it is selected or can be conceivably thought of as selected by a preposition, and when it is the complement of any verb except *be:*

> *Whom* did you apply to?
> Men *whom* I knew did this crime.

In the first of those examples, the grammatical status of *whom* is by no means clear. The stress on *to* would indicate that it is grammatically a directive adverb, not a preposition, and directive adverbs cannot force a pronoun into the "objective" case form, least of all a pronoun which is separated from them by the entire context of a sentence. The *whom* in the second example is unusual as being a complement *preceding* its subject and verb. Thus the entire pressure of the language is thrown against its continued use. There can be no doubt that crucial instances such as those are gradually leading to a deliberate avoidance of language situations in which *whom* could be used. When speakers and writers become afraid of a grammatical form, they replace it, in this example by nothing—except the all-important implications of fixed word order.

9.20   The confusions examined in 9.18 and 9.19 have had lamentable effect on the writing and speech of superficially educated persons. They have led directly to improprieties more blameworthy than the minor grammatical divergencies that prompted them:

a. The use of the direct forms of pronouns where the indirect forms are obviously needed:

> They gave *John and I* the book.
> Between *you and I,* I can't agree with his theory.

b. The use of *whom* where *who* is obviously needed:

> Would you tell me *whom* ought to be told?

The motivation for these linguistic gargoyles lies partly in fear and partly in snobbishness. Constant correction of the "objective" forms of pronouns in favor of the "nominative" forms has created the curious notion that these "objective" forms are intrinsically inelegant. Naturally enough, the unfortunates cursed with this notion avoid such forms as much as possible. A return to the clear principles of spoken English, or better, the adoption of a realistic grammar of written English, seems overdue.

9.21   On this note, the rapid survey of English word-group principles attempted here can conveniently close. The fact is, in a language so fluid in its essential nature as English, so simple in outline and so varied in detail, there is no real excuse for a writer's becoming embroiled with minor difficulties of usage. There is always an alternative construction ready to his hand. Naturally, as he passes out of his first apprenticeship to the written language, the contrasts between alternative constructions and the need for more and more of them become real to him. One cannot walk before learning to crawl. Time and constant practice will be required before the full resources of English grammatical structure are at anyone's service. Nevertheless, this is the English language—our own language. Like any other skill, the skill of writing it well can be acquired.

10 The system of punctuation

10.1 The traditional purpose of punctuation is to symbolize by means of visual signs the patterns heard in speech. Grammarians of the eighteenth century, strongly conscious of pause but little observant of tone and juncture, thought that the comma indicated pause for a time count of one, the semicolon for a time count of two, the colon for a time count of three, and the period for a time count of four. Nowadays, we know that pause is simply pause, that pause is often optional, and that when present it combines with preceding junctures to build up what may be regarded as an audible punctuation of words, word-groups, and sentences when we are speaking. To these combinations of speech phenomena, the common punctuation marks of writing (.), (?), (;), (—), (,) bear a correlation which is at best only approximate. Moreover, modern English punctuation has become an intricate system of conventions, some logical, some indicating separations or connections of context, all of crucial practical importance. Its most important purpose is "to make grammar graphic." As a kind of visual configurational feature of grammar (2.2), punctuation cannot be properly understood unless the other grammatical features of the language are also understood.

10.2 Punctuation is employed in the following functions:

a. To *link* sentences and parts of words.

b. To *separate* sentences and parts of sentences.

c. To *enclose* parts of sentences.

d. To *indicate* omissions.

We can thus speak of *linking, separating, enclosing,* and *omission* punctuation in the full realization that each function contrasts directly with all the others. It follows, therefore, that when the same marks of punctuation are used in different functions they are very much like words used in different functions: the grammatical meanings of the marks are *different*. The *separating period* (.) is quite distinct in functional use from the *omission period* (.); the *linking dash* (−) is functionally distinct from the *omission dash* (−); the single *separating comma* (,) is functionally distinct from *enclosing commas* (, . . . ,). In an ideal punctuation system, such differences would be clarified by the use of different marks of punctuation. Yet let us be realistic. Man has been speaking for well over 700,000 years. Man has been practicing alphabetic writing only for about 3450 years. Man has punctuated, in the modern sense, for less than 250 years. He has still not mastered an ideal punctuation. In the system as it stands, the distribution of the marks is as follows:

a. For *linking,* use:
  ;   the semicolon
  :   the colon
  −   the linking dash
  -   the linking hyphen

b. For *separating,* use:
  .   the period
  ?   the question mark
  !   the exclamation point
  ,   the separating comma

c. For *enclosing,* use:

, . . . , paired commas

— . . . — paired dashes

(. . .) paired parentheses

[. . .] paired brackets

" . . . " paired quotation marks

d. For *indicating omissions,* use:

' the apostrophe

. the omission period (or dot)

— the omission dash

. . . triple periods (or dots)

. . . . quadruple periods (or dots)

10.3 Linking punctuation. The semicolon (;), colon (:), and dash (—) are symbolic conjunctions capable of linking subject-predicate constructions without need of conjunctions proper. They differ chiefly in the way they direct emphasis. Semicolons distribute it more or less equally between preceding and following statements; colons throw it forwards towards following statements; dashes throw it backwards towards preceding statements. Since they function as symbolic conjunctions, none of these marks is associated with any distinctive tone pattern of the language. In most cases, indeed, statements preceding any one of them would be read with the final h—l tone-pause pattern characteristic of period punctuation. The hyphen differs from the other linking punctuation marks in that it is used to link parts of the words only. The semicolon, colon, and dash may occur in combination with a final quotation mark, in which case they are always placed *outside* the quotation mark.

10.4 The *semicolon* (;) is the symbolic conjunction used to link subject-predicate groups that could otherwise occur as separate sentences, particularly if they are parallel in structure and in emphasis:

> The girl is pretty; you will like her.
> I am out of work; I need financial help.

I was ill that day; nevertheless, I tried to complete the work.

He was a close friend of the family; moreover, he had a position open.

It is conventionally used to link word groups containing heavy internal comma punctuation:

My outfit included a rifle, a shotgun, a water bag, and a bedroll; but I did not forget to include a few good books.

I liked *The Ordeal of Richard Feverel,* by Meredith; *Oliver Twist,* by Dickens; and Oscar Wilde's fine comedy *The Importance of Being Earnest.*

When the semicolon occurs in conjunction with quotation marks, it is placed *outside* them:

I was reading Shelley's "Adonais"; I did not wish to be disturbed.

10.5 The *colon* (:) is the symbolic conjunction used when emphasis is to be thrown forward upon the word-group or word that follows it:

It was just as I thought: he had stolen the money.

My outfit included these necessaries: a rifle, a shotgun, a water bag, and a bedroll.

I could think of only one word to describe him: cad.

In keeping with its general function of *anticipation,* the colon is conventionally used to introduce the chapter figure of a Bible reference, the page number of a volume reference, the minute figure of a clock reference, and the body of a letter following the salutation:

> Numbers III: 21 (or 3:21)
> American Speech 12: 46-49
> 10:15 A.M.
> Dear Sir:

Like the semicolon, it is always placed *outside* a final quotation mark:

I found one leading literary tradition in "Adonais": pastoral tone.

10.6 The *dash* (—) is the symbolic conjunction to be used when the word-group or word following it is considered to be subsidiary to, a reinforcement or example of, or an unexpected addition to what precedes it. It directs the reader's attention backward:

A year's work at Harvard—that was what he hoped for.
A rifle, shotgun, ammunition—these were the essentials of my outfit.
He comes to dinner, eats your food, smokes your best cigars—then borrows your money.
He was very crude—crude and utterly crazy.

The dash is conventionally used before the name of the author of a quotation:

> Here lies our sovereign lord, the King.
> Whose word no man relies on;
> Who never spoke a foolish thing,
> And never did a wise one.
>
> —Anonymous

The dash should *not* be used as a kind of coverall punctuation mark for all linking and separating functions.

10.7 The *hyphen* (-) links parts of words together. It is most characteristically used to indicate that contiguous words form compounds not marked by stress modification (12.4, 12.8).

> a *well-beloved* woman
> my *commander-in-chief*
> his *better-than-thou* attitude

The conventional uses of the hyphen are these:

a. To indicate that the beginning of a word on one printed line is linked to the rest of the word on the next.

b. To link the elements of compound numbers from twenty-one to ninety-nine:

thirty-four horses
sixty-seven dollars

c. To link the elements of fractions:

He had a *two-thirds* lead in the election.

Today we tend to write either separately or as single units those words which were formerly hyphenated:

my *commander in chief*
a *wellbred* woman

10.8 Separating punctuation. The period separates sentences only. The exclamation mark (!) and the question mark (?), normally used to separate special types of sentences, are also used occasionally to separate parts of sentences. The comma separates *parts* of sentences only. Thus, there is every reason why the period, as sentences separator, should never be confused with the comma, as sentence-part separator, or with the semicolon, the sentence linker. All the separating punctuation marks are roughly correlated with stress-juncture and tone-pause patterns heard in speech, and it is probable that learning to hear the patterns will direct you towards the appropriate punctuation:

John was coming(.)
John was coming(?)
John was coming(!)
John was coming(,) and I still had to dress.

When they occur in combination with final quotation marks, all the separating punctuation marks are placed *inside* them. In this respect, they contrast directly with the linking punctuation marks which are placed *outside*.

10.9 The period (.) has the one function of separating declarative subject-predicate sentences
(including mild commands) from following sentences. It
symbolizes the fall from high to low pitch (h—l) followed
by breathing pause. Its grammatical meaning is "end of
declarative utterance":

> The mountains enclose a valley.
> Please return the books as soon as possible.

The period can occur after statements not in subject-
predicate form if they conclude with the h—l tone-pause
pattern.

> The more, the merrier.
> To resume.

It is always inserted *before* end quotation marks:

> He said to me, "Mother is coming."

10.10 The question mark (?) separates questions and
quoted questions from a following context. It
symbolizes two quite distinct final tone-pause patterns
of actual speech:

a. A fall from high to low tone (h—l) used when a
question contains an interrogative word or word order:

> h————l
> Why did you go to the theater?

b. A rising high tone, usual when a question does not
contain an interrogative word or word order:

> h————l
> You went to the theater?

The grammatical meaning of the question mark is "answer needed":

> Are you leaving tonight?
> Is John coming?
> You are in Professor Brown's class?
> "Where is the salt?" he demanded.

It is always inserted *before* end quotation marks:

> He said, "Is this what's wrong?"

10.11 The *exclamation point* (!) separates exclamatory sentences or exclamatory words from a following context. It symbolizes various final tone-pause patterns based upon sharply rising or falling tone or a combination of these, or unexpectedly level tone, used in speech when an utterance is surcharged with emotion:

> What a marvelous morning!
> Listen! I hear John coming.

It is always inserted *before* end quotation marks that occur *within* a sentence, but it is placed outside quotation marks at the end of a sentence when the whole sentence is exclamatory:

"I am finished!" he yelled.
How horrible was their shout, "We're coming to kill you"!

10.12 The *separating comma* (,) originally indicated that a part of a sentence preceding or following it was in some way separated from the remainder. Where it corresponds to anything in speech at all, it generally symbolizes internal grammatical juncture followed by pause in slow-tempo speech (2.24.b). Its use, however, is now highly conventionalized: the comma is often used where speech shows internal juncture unaccompanied by pause but where its omission might lead to misunderstanding. The comma never appears between the main structural elements, the *must* parts, of sentences; i.e., it is never used between the subject and verb, between the verb and a complement, or between two complements, and it is never used before movable modifiers of a sentence if these appear *after* the verb; in short, it is never used to indicate optional internal grammatical junctures. The grammatical meaning of the comma is "dissociation." It is inserted:

a. After each word or word-group in a series terminated by *and, or;* here it may symbolize the high rising tone pattern (h):

I took bread, butter, tea, and salt with me.
His cunning, his devious treachery, or his ruthlessness will be enough to make him fight successfully.

b. Between subject-predicate word-groups linked by the coupling conjunctions *and, but, or, not, yet:*

The book is quite good, and it is relatively inexpensive.
The food and service were good, yet I was hard to please.

c. After any movable modifier (4.7) thought of as displaced from a normal end-of-sentence position:

Instead of the expected twenty, only ten came to the party.
But: Only ten came to the party instead of the expected twenty.

d. Before any other modifier or modifying word-group thought of as out of its normal sentence position:

We thought of Goldsmith, poor but genial.
Talent, Mr. Micawber has; money, Mr. Micawber has not.

e. After an introductory word, word-group, transitional adverb, or vocative expression:

This done, we left the place immediately.
She didn't like the idea; *nevertheless,* she said she would visit us.
Mother, I have brought my friend to be our guest.

f. After a subject-predicate word-group introducing a direct quotation:

He exclaimed, "I had no idea that you were in the room."

g. Between elements in sentences and word-groups which might cause confusion if thought of as combined:

My words are my own; my actions, my ministers'.
a bright, blue hat contrasted with a *bright blue hat*

h. Between items in dates, addresses, books and author references, etc.:

> April 1, 1950
> Mary Johnson, Cleveland, Ohio
> *Oliver Twist,* by Charles Dickens

The comma is always inserted *before* end quotation marks:

> "I am tired of your incompetence," he roared.

10.13 Enclosing punctuation. Paired commas, paired dashes, and parentheses are used to enclose elements outside the main structure of a sentence. They represent a triple scale of enclosure, in which paired commas enclose elements most closely related to the main thought of the sentence and parentheses those elements least closely related. Brackets are merely a specialized type of parentheses. Quotation marks are used principally to enclose the report of words actually spoken.

10.14 *Paired commas* (, . . . ,) have the following uses:

a. To enclose modifying word-groups of the subject-predicate type which are not regarded as essential to the identification of the word which they modify. Such groups are usually called *non-restrictive*. (For details of the *who/which* subject-predicate group, see 5.17).

NON-RESTRICTIVE: This invention, *which our army rejected,* became Germany's surprise weapon.

RESTRICTIVE: The invention *which our army rejected* became Germany's surprise weapon.

In the first example, the identification is supplied by *this;* the modifying group *which our army rejected* is thus properly enclosed in paired commas. In the second example, the modifying group is needed to identify *invention.*

b. To enclose interpolated words and word-groups, especially when those are transitional adverbs (5.20) or groups with the function of transitional adverbs:

> Your ideas, *however,* are scarcely valid.
> Your ideas, *as a matter of fact,* are scarcely valid.
> Yours ideas, *I conclude,* are scarcely valid.

10.15 *Paired dashes* (— . . . —) enclose elements less closely related to the main thought of a sentence than those enclosed by paired commas but more closely related than those enclosed by parentheses:

My friends—at that time mostly workers—took me to task for my social attitudes.

They replace paired commas when the enclosed word-group has heavy comma punctuation of its own:

The artillery—devastating in its sound, fury, and effect—suddenly opened up on us.

10.16 Parentheses enclose material which is obviously outside the main scope of the sentence:

These words (*we might call them determiners*) are important in English but of little importance in many other languages.

Parentheses are used conventionally to enclose the figures numbering parts of a series, and, in legal contexts, to enclose figures expressing monetary value:

The aims of this course are: (1) to analyze the structure of American English; (2) to examine the resources of its vocabulary; (3) to sketch the history of American English.

The signer agrees to pay the sum of one hundred dollars ($100.00).

10.17 Brackets ([. . .]) are a special kind of parentheses with the following uses:

a. To insert interpolations in quotations:

As Jarrold said, "It [poetry] is an attempt to express the inexpressible."

b. To insert pronunciations written in the symbols of the International Phonetic Association (IPA):

The usual pronunciation of *bait* is [bet].

They also enclose parenthetical matter already in parentheses.

10.18 *Quotation marks* (" . . . ") enclose direct quotations from speech:

"You may say that," said my father, "but you don't believe it."

They may be used with caution to enclose references to specific words, slang expressions, hackneyed expressions, familiar and well-worn phrases, and terms you do not like:

My life is one "if" after another.
His car had the "teardrop" shape of that period.
While "on campus," Jones was something of a "rod."
The "liberal arts" curriculum becomes increasingly illiberal.

They are also used to enclose the titles of poems, plays, essays, paintings, etc. (but not the titles of complete volumes or of major works, which are indicated by italics):

I read Shelley's "Alastor" with distinct pleasure.
I particularly admired El Greco's "Toledo."
He was much impressed by the story "Clay" in Joyce's *Dubliners*.

10.19 Omission punctuation. Originally, the *apostrophe* (') indicated the omission of a letter no longer pronounced or deliberately suppressed in pronunciation. This is what it still indicates when used with the possessive singular forms of nouns, contracted forms of verb helpers (auxiliaries), and words with an omitted initial letter:

> the Lord's Prayer (earlier, the Lordes Prayer)
> He's not coming, and he won't come.
> a blot on the 'scutcheon

Its conventional uses are as follows:

a. It precedes *s* in the plurals of figures, signs, symbols, and letters:

> My 8's are difficult to decipher.
> There were three x's in this quotation.
> I have difficulty in writing r's.

b. It precedes *s* in plurals of words which have no normal plural form:

> There were too many if's and but's about the matter.

c. In a purely symbolic function corresponding to nothing actual in speech, it indicates possessive plurals of nouns:

> The generals' orders had to be obeyed.
> the college girls' escorts

d. It indicates the possessive singular forms of nouns already ending in *s:*

> Dr. Caius' (or Caius's) words
> Moses' pronouncements

e. It indicates the possessive singular forms of group names:

> Thomas, Manchester, and Scott's *Rhetoric*
> Chase and Sanborn's coffee

f. It indicates the omission of initial centuries in dates:

the class of '38

10.20 The *omission period* or *dot* (.) indicates the omission of several letters, particularly when words are abbreviated:

> Mr. V. S. Johnson
> Ph.D.
> I enjoy the plays of G.B.S.

It is not used after contractions indicated by the apostrophe, after Roman numerals, after numbered ordinals, after nicknames, or after per cent (for *per centum*); it is now often omitted after the abbreviated names of government agencies, labor organizations, and the like:

> He'll go.
> XXIV
> 5th, 6th, 7th
> Dick, Mick, and Ned
> a five per cent bonus
> CIC
> FTC

When a sentence ends with an abbreviated word, one period punctuates both the abbreviation and the sentence:

> I was talking to Richard Hudson, Ph.D.

10.21 *Triple periods* or *dots* (. . .) indicate a more or less extensive omission of material at the beginning of, or within, a quoted passage; followed by a period (. . . .) they indicate omission at its end:

. . . language is . . . the thought itself, its confused cross currents as well as its clear-cut issues. . . .

Triple periods are often used to indicate omissions deliberately left to the reader's imagination:

He took her slowly in his arms . . . from that moment she was his.

In recent advertising practice, this use is greatly extended in order to create appropriate atmosphere:

Fly to Britain . . . Europe . . . and beyond.
Industries are discovering . . . with a rush . . . that the Genie of "Opportunity" is at their beck and call.

10.22 The *dash* (–) as used in omission punctuation indicates the deliberate suppression of letters in a person's name in order to avoid positive statement of identification:

My informant, a certain professor *M*–, vouches for the truth of this report.

In earlier writing it was often used to indicate omissions in oaths, etc.:

"D–n," he said. "I'll see you hanged yet."

10.23 No attempt has been made here to deal with all the minute points of punctuation. Such matters as the use of capitals and italics are treated under the appropriate headings in a dictionary: they are matters of format rather than punctuation although they serve a very real purpose in the transference of spoken to written distinctions (2.22–2.24). What has been attempted here is to present punctuation proper as a system of symbols each one of which contrasts with all others in function. Ideally, the writer should be able to ignore the grammar book or the dictionary when he is faced with a punctuation problem; what he needs most of all is an understanding of the entire system as it determines the individual application.

11 | Spelling and pronunciation

11.1 The trouble with modern English spelling is
that it does not spell modern English. It does
not even approximately spell modern English. What it
does spell is the English of the Late Middle English
period around 1470 A.D. Ironically enough, it represents
the pronunciation of that period with such accuracy that
a student of the English language can tell from the spelling of today exactly how words were uttered in the
London area of England during the late fifteenth century. What is even more ironical, the best way in which
to learn how to pronounce the words of such earlier writers as Chaucer is to respell them in the modern English
fashion and pronounce accordingly. Such features as our
"silent" *e*, our erratic doubling of consonants, and our
"silent" *gh* are highly significant, but for Middle, not for
Modern English. The first originally indicated either
that the preceding vowel was a "long" one (as in *mane*,
life, home) or that the preceding consonant was a "soft"
one (as in *tinge, tingeing, advantage*); the second showed
that the preceding vowel was a short one (as in *bitt, batt,
butter*); the third symbolized the friction consonant now
lost in English but still heard in German *Nacht, Bach,
Loch,* etc. All this is vastly interesting to the historian of
English and to the etymologist; to the ordinary person

of the twentieth century it is a tragic muddle. If modern English could be spelled not as perfectly as Finnish but as relatively imperfectly as German or French, millions of man-hours could be saved each year in our educational institutions alone—man-hours that ought to be devoted to far more important matters of learning.

11.2 Yet, nothing very practical can be done about English spelling. Although linguists have devised a spelling system which accurately reflects pronunciation, to adopt it generally would be premature if not impossible. Even if we were willing to shoulder the enormous financial burden of reprinting all books and newspapers in this system, we should still have to come to terms with the great series of changes in pronunciation that commenced in the fifteenth century and are still proceeding. Already, in many parts of the United States, the vowel of *moon, spoon* has moved to a position halfway between that of $\overline{oo}$ and $\overline{ee}$, while that of *good* is halfway between *oo* and *i*. Today's English is not the English of tomorrow nor of the day after tomorrow. If our generation should, by some miracle, decide to adopt the scientific spelling system of the linguists, it would have to face the possibility of modifications, perhaps basic modifications, some two or three generations hence. Meanwhile, such spelling reforms as *thru* for *through, nite* for *night,* and *enuf* for *enough,* although they do no particular harm, do no particular good. They merely fringe the central problem of English spelling. The most practical step we could take would be to de-emphasize spelling both educationally and socially and throw it back into the hands of its proper legal guardians, the printers and the publishers. This is not a new idea. It was advocated by the late Professor Child of Harvard. It recognizes the fact that regularized spelling is primarily a matter of concern for printers, that many well-educated writers of the seventeenth and eighteenth centuries cared very little for spelling, that the cult of correct spelling as a sign of literacy was one of the many linguistic insecurities developed during the period of social insecurity known as the Industrial Revolution.

11.3 Anyone who reads much and possesses a good visual memory will reproduce the accepted spellings of English words a great deal of the time. Anyone who reads little, writes less, and possesses a predominantly audile memory will spell acceptably very little of the time. Both will, in either case, be obliged to consult the dictionary rather frequently. No one, no matter how learned, can spell all of the more than 700,000 words constituting the English language today; nor is he expected to. Yet any person who allows his writing to reach a reader without having checked doubtful spellings is rash, careless, or foolish. The more untrustworthy his spelling, the more checking with the dictionary he must do; the more trustworthy his spelling, the less checking he will need. Good spelling, then, has one positive advantage: it saves trouble. On occasions when no dictionary is handy, it can also save social embarrassment. For some professional people, such as the secretaries of important business, administrative, or educational executives, it is of course a necessity. In their case an early encephalographic test might be of great diagnostic use.

11.4 The best way to learn to spell is to write a great deal and to read much more. Spelling is learned by doing, and by subconscious impressions imprinted by constant repetition. Since English spelling is so completely arbitrary—irreducible to a correspondence of single sound to single letter as in Finnish or to recurrent groups of letters as in French—we are forced to rely upon an indirect and haphazard method of mastering it. But if the method fails and we still want to write, we should never let the feeling that we cannot spell prevent us from writing. A knowledge of the interlocking syntactical patterns of English—its devices for building words, its rhythmic patterns—is ultimately far more important than acceptable spelling alone. There have been many famous writers of English in our own and earlier generations whose spelling was, by all conventional standards, atrocious; there are millions of "good" spellers who cannot and never will write anything worth reading. If spelling comes hard, it is a good plan when writing not to worry much about it until the final draft—the draft to which the cleaning up of spelling, like the cleaning up of style, properly belongs. Above all, let us avoid developing an inferiority complex about spelling.

11.5 Ideally, from the beginnings of his education, a student of English should learn to spell it in a scientific way, first by being taught the basic sound system of the language, then by associating each sound with the commonest method of spelling it and then by learning the less common or exceptional methods of spelling it. After all, imperfect as English spelling is, the distributional occurrence of forms in contexts, or, to put it in another way, the "sense" of the language situation, is the clearest clue to spelling. Thus *meat, meet,* and *mete* are in sound exactly alike. Yet the first occurs only as a noun, the second as verb and noun in entirely different contexts from the first, and the latter only in the two expressions *mete out* and *metes and bounds.* Like all other languages, English is fundamentally a patterned, segmented, and rhythmed code of voice signals (1.1). To this code, a perfect spelling system would correspond exactly, symbolizing each voice signal by a single, unambiguous written sign. No written sign would symbolize two signals, as do the *g* of *good* and the *g* of *gin,* and no two signs would symbolize one signal, like the *s* of *sieve* and the *c* of *receive.* The correspondences between the sound structure and the spelling structure would be absolute. The result would be a *phonemic spelling system,* i.e., a system of spelling which accurately reflected all the sound signals used in the language to differentiate one meaning from another.

11.6 Such a system actually exists and has been used by linguistic specialists for some time. Various versions of it may serve different purposes—this for work on dialects, that for the study of word-formation, another for the study of the basic structure of the language. The following version, which the writer has found to be simple and effective in the description of the sound signals of most varieties of American English, consists of thirty-one signs symbolizing thirty-one recurrent sound signals (*phonemes*) of the language. Most of these signs are drawn from the standard alphabet; five of them (θ, ð, ŋ, ə, æ) are taken from the alphabet of the International Phonetic Association. They are grouped below (Fig. 10) roughly by phonetic type and according to their articulation by the lower lip or some part of the tongue.

11.7 Before this system can be practically used, certain other points must be clearly understood:

a. English has a few recurrent clusters of sonants with semivowels, i.e., of a vowel sound together with /y/, a glide towards the front of the tongue; or /h/, a glide towards the center of the tongue; or /w/, a glide towards the back of the tongue. These are the traditional "long vowels" of the language including the sounds actually heard in *beet* /biyt/, *bate* /beyt/, *bite* /bayt/, *bout* /bawt/ or /bæwt/, *boy* /boy/, *boat* /bowt/ or /bɔwt/, *boot* /buwt/, as well as *bird* /bəhrd/ or /bəhd/ (or, as substandard in New York City and ordinary with many fine speakers in the South /bəyd/).

b. The key words *pot* and *salt* with /a/ and /o/ may be misleading for some speakers of American English. Those in New England, for instance, may have /o/ rather than /a/ in *pot*. The same is true of speakers from Western Pennsylvania and from the river territories into

Figure 10

ENGLISH PHONEMES

	Lip	Tongue Apex	Tongue Front	Tongue Center	Tongue Back
CONSONANTS:					
A. *Obstructives*					
1. Stopped	p	t	č (*ch*est)		k
	b	d	ǰ (*j*est)		g
2. Frictional	f	θ (*th*in)			
	v	ð (*th*en)			
3. Sibilant		s	š (*sh*ip)		
		z	ž (a*z*ure)		
B. *Resonants*					
4. Nasalized	m	n			ŋ (si*ng*)
5. Vowel-like		r			
		l			
6. Semivowels			y	h	w
SONANTS (VOWELS):					
1. Tongue high			i (p*i*t)		u (p*u*t)
2. Tongue inter-mediate			e (p*e*t)	ə (b*u*t)	o (s*a*lt)
3. Tongue low			æ (p*a*t)		a (p*o*t)

which the Western Pennsylvania influence has penetrated. On the other hand, speakers from certain other areas may have /a/ in *salt,* particularly in the Rocky Mountain areas, in which *cot* and *caught* are both /kat/.

c. Lengthened vowels, which occur in American English usually when the resonants *r, l* and a back consonant /x/, spelled -gh, have dropped out of pronunciation, are usually interpreted as elements consisting of a sonant (vowel) phoneme followed by /h/. Thus, common pronunciations of *bought, talk* would be /boht/, /tohk/ just as the Eastern pronunciations of *hard, scorn, bird* would sometimes be /hahd/, /skohn/, /bəhd/.

11.8 From these points, it follows that the use of a phonemic alphabet leaves room for some individual variation. A Southerner might write /biwt/, /bæwt/, /bahd/, /bəhd/ or /bəyd/ for *boot, bout, bide, bird*. A person from the North Central West would probably write /buwt/, /bawt/, /bayd/, /bəhrd/. And rightly so. Although a fixed spelling system may lighten the toil of editors, publishers, lexicographers, and glossarizers, one's speech heritage is not something to be lightly cast aside—especially when, as in the United States, its reflection in phonemic spelling cannot conceivably cause difficulties of understanding. There is not, and—unless a human miracle happens—never will be, a "standard" American spelling. Language communicates; among other things, it communicates personality. What I say or write is, to a large degree, *me,* even if it is a *me* processing what I say or write according to the system of the language. One of the greatest—and hitherto unrealized—advantages of phonemic spelling is that it would allow *me* to be generally known as my own personality, not only through the higher levels of word-group manipulation and choice of words but also in my choice of sound signals (phonemes) themselves: /not ownli θru ðə hayər levelz əv wəhrdgruwp mænipyulešən ənd čoys əv wəhrdz/bət ohlsow in may čoys əv sawndsignəlz ðəmselvz/. But this, presumably, is a dream of a roseate and perhaps impossible future when knowledge of language has replaced fear of language.

12 Word-formation

12.1 In writing, words are recognized as words by the spacing. Spoken words are recognized as words only because the speaker and hearer are familiar with the total design of the language (nowadays including its conventions of writing). In this recognition, four speech factors seem to be of importance:

a. Every word is likely to occur at some time in some contexts before and after juncture.

b. Many words mark their beginnings and endings by phonetic boundary signals (phonemic variants; allophones). Contrast *that's tough,* where the initial /t/ is aspirated (i.e., followed by a slight breath explosion) with *that stuff,* where /t/ after /s/ is not aspirated; contrast *that's odd,* where /s/ is very slightly articulated, with *that sod* where the initial /s/ is strongly articulated.

c. Some words mark their beginnings and endings by cluster boundary signals, i.e., they begin or end with clusters of consonants which are commonly found in word-initial or word-final positions (e.g., /spl-/ as in *split,* /-rts/ as in *quartz*).

d. Many words mark their beginnings and endings with prefixes and suffixes (12.5).

In general, English more insistently marks the beginnings and endings of word-groups and of syllables (stretches of utterance which are the domains of a particular stress, see 2.23) than of individual words. This is in keeping with its general grammatical nature as a word-group language.

12.2 The usual, quite unsatisfactory definition of *word* is "a minimum unit of meaning." If "meaning" here implies only *practical* meaning, then empty words cannot be words at all. If "meaning" includes *grammatical* meaning, then the last phoneme /t/ of *chased* /čeys-t/, which has the grammatical meaning of "past time," is a word—as it undoubtedly is not. Either way, the definition is worthless. Actually, the real "minimum unit of meaning" may be a word (*dog*), a syllable (-*ly* in *quickly*, -*ing* in *singing*), or a single phoneme (/t/ in *chased*). This minimum unit, no matter how constituted, is known as a *morpheme*. It is a free *morpheme* (free form) if it can appear as a word (e.g., *dog*), a *bound morpheme* if in all occurrences it is attached to other morphemes (e.g., -*ly* in *quickly*, -*ing* in *singing*, /t/ in *chased*).

12.3 Morphemes, whether free or bound, can be manipulated in certain specific ways to build up new words or to change the grammatical forms of words. Such built-up words are either *compounds* or *derivatives*. English words, therefore, can be classified by structure as *morpheme words, compounds,* and *derivatives,* just as by function they can be classified as *full words, empty words,* and *substitute words.*

12.4 Compounding. Free morphemes combine to form compounds: *dogday* (from *dog* and *day*), *blackbird* (from *black* and *bird*), *sweetbread* (from *sweet* and *bread*), etc. Most of these compounds crystallize by a natural linguistic process from word-groups and are invariably accompanied by *stress modification* (12.8).

12.5 Affixing. Bound morphemes combine with other morphemes to form derivatives. Such words can be analyzed into a base preceded or followed by an affix. If the affix precedes its base, it is a *prefix;* if it follows, it is a *suffix.* The base may be a free morpheme (*man* in *manly*), a compound (*horseman* in *horseman-ship*), a derivative word (*gentlemanly* in *gentlemanliness*), or another bound morpheme (*-ceive* in *receive, deceive, perceive*).

12.6 **Zeroing.** In mathematical series of the negative-positive type, zero is a number:

$$-3, \ -2, \ -1, \ 0, \ 1, \ 2, \ 3$$

So also in language. The absence of addition to or change in a form may have important implications. Thus the lack of the suffix *-s* in he *will, shall, can, may, need, dare* denotes "non-actuality." Similarly, the lack of *-s* in *I went out after deer* (*bear, quail, partridge, trout, salmon*) means something like "non-distinctive number." Such forms are *zero derivatives.*

12.7 **Internal modification.** Phonemes within a word may be replaced by others to convey changes of meaning or function. Thus to *gild* /gild/ is to apply *gold* /gowld/ to something; *milk* /milk/ is obtained from *milch cows* /milč/; the plural of *goose* /guws/ is *geese* /giys/ and the plural of *foot* /fut/ is *feet* /fiyt/; the past tense form of *break* /breyk/ is *broke* /browk/; during your *life* /layf/ you *live* /liv/. Internal modification is frequently combined with affixing (12.5) in derivatives seldom recognized as such by casual observers. The combination is apparent in *stealth* /stelθ/ from *steal,* and *health* /helθ/ from *heal;* it is much less apparent in *filth* /filθ/ from *foul* /fawl/, *sleuth* /sluwθ/ from *sly* /slay/, *vixen* /viks-ən/ from *fox* /faks/, *ready* /red-iy/ from *ride* /rayd/, and *next* /nek-st/ from *nigh* /nay/.

12.8 **Stress modification.** The basic contrast of falling versus rising stress pattern has widespread applications in word formation (see 2.17–2.19):

a. It distinguishes the noun use of certain two-morpheme words from the verbal use: *ínlay*, *inláy*; *ímpact*, *impáct*; *áddress*, *addréss*. (stress marks [s])

b. It distinguishes compounds from word-groups of the same form: *bláckbird* versus *bláck bírd*, *whítewash* versus *whíte wásh*, *récord pláyer* (a phonograph) versus *recórd pláyer* (a player who breaks records in games), etc.

c. It distinguishes full and substitute word compounds from empty word compounds: contrast *whítewash*, *séed péarl*, *sómeone*, *sómewhere* with *withín*, *withóut*, *upón*, *untíl*.

d. It distinguishes compounds proper from quasi-compounds: contrast *cútback*, *bréakthrough*, *thrówout*, all based upon a verb plus directive, with *well-bréd*, *well-cút*, *clíp-fed*, *machíne-made*, all derivatives based upon verb plus qualifier or qualifying word-group.

The actual formative function of stress modification is to make nouns from verbs and noun word-groups by reversing the stress pattern.

12.9 Reduplication. In some languages, morphemes are systematically doubled to indicate number, tense, and the like. In English, such doubling is rare and, apart from the children's word *choo-choo*, always combined with internal modification (12.7):

tip-tap	*pitter-patter*	*helter-skelter*
riff-raff	*fiddle-faddle*	*harum-scarum*
criss-cross	*wishy-washy*	*namby-pamby*

12.10 Replacement. Most languages possess a few morphemes obviously identified in meaning with other morphemes but showing no conceivable phonetic connection with them. Such morphemes are construed as *replacing* the morphemes with which they are so closely associated. In English, replacement appears in the use of *went* (from the verb *wend*) as the past tense form of *go,* and in the use of *am, is, are, was, were,* as parts of the verb *be.* It is also present in the system of personal substitutes: *I, me; we, us; she, her.*

12.11 Compounding, affixing, zeroing, internal modification, stress modification, reduplication, and replacement together constitute the word-building (*morphological*) processes of English. Theoretically, if you understand their operation you will be capable of analyzing into its constituents any compound or derivative in the language. In practice, analysis is by no means easy.

12.12 The fact is, compounds and derivatives in the English vocabulary fall into two classes: (1) those transparent in formation; (2) those obscure. In the former class, words built up by the *active* word-building devices and *active* affixes are quite clearly formed from constituent morphemes which have themselves a clear, usually invariable, form: i.e., *re-enter, post-doctoral, anti-Fascist, belittle, blackbird, un-American.* Within the limits of this *active morphology,* the utmost complexity you can expect is furnished by the behavior of the suffix *-(e)s* in its three variant forms:

A	B	C	D
bit-s /s/	he hit-s /s/	Harriet's /s/	He works night-s. /s/
rod-z /z/	he ride-s /z/	Maud's /z/	He works weekend-s. /z/
house-s /ǝz/	he cross-es /ǝz/	Bess's /ǝz/	He works Christmas-es /ǝz/

Even here, the variants are predictable: /s/, /z/, or /ǝz/ appear according as the last consonant of the base is voiceless, voiced, or sibilant.

12.13 The second class of compounds and derivatives roughly comprises words embodying *non-active* word-building devices and affixes, compounds long established in the language, and derivatives borrowed from French, Latin, Greek, and other languages. Here, the difficulties of analysis are not uniformly severe, for some of the words show relatively slight formal or morphemic modification (*man, men; goose, geese; heal, health; filter, filtrate*) and in others the underlying morphemes are preserved by the spelling: *clapboard*/klabərd/, *boatswain*/bowsən/, *waistcoat*/weskət/, *forehead*/fored/. But, in general, such words obscure their formation by bewildering alternations of form in bases and affixes, by interaction between neighboring phonemes, and by the inclusion of bound morpheme bases whose meanings are undecipherable from English alone. Few speakers of English are aware that the common prefix *ad-* is the first morpheme of *accrue, affix, aggravate, allocate, announce, applaud, arrange, assist,* and *attract.* Fewer still would associate *ready* with its base *ride,* or guess the meaning of the bound base *-ceive* in *receive, deceive, perceive.* It seems fair to say that such words are used and understood as wholes irrespective of their constituents, whereas the words of the active morphology can be and probably are understood in terms of the morphemes composing them.

12.14 We can profit much by breaking down words into their constituents with the help of a good etymological dictionary. In so doing, we learn that whole segments of the English vocabulary interlock in form and meaning, and that words, like the elements of the atomic table, may transmute into each other through change of internal structure.

Appendix

A.1 If education in the ways of American English were realistic, every citizen of our democracy would be able to make at least partial answers to the two crucial questions:

1. What is the American English language?
2. From what did it develop?

The preceding chapters have attempted to answer some facets of the first question. Although the second question is outside the scope of this book, some observations about it in connection with written English will not be out of place.

A.2 A generalized written English first came into prominence during the late fourteenth and early fifteenth centuries on the basis of a single spoken dialect of the language. The dialect was that of London and the South East Midland counties, partly as written in the administrative, governmental, ecclesiastical, and legal offices (London Official English), partly as used in trade from the mercantile towns of East Anglia, partly as employed in literature by Chaucer, Gower, Occleve, Lydgate, and other writers, and perhaps most significantly, as magnificently handled in sermons and influential mystical treatises. These four strands—the official, the mercantile, the literary, and the religious—have been active factors in shaping its development ever since. The first attempts to standardize its spelling, grammar, and vocabulary came from the practical needs of early printing, naively summarized by Caxton in the following famous passage:

> And certainly our language as now used varieth far from that which was used and spoken when I was born. For we Englishmen be born under the domination of the moon, which is never steadfast, but ever wavering, waxing one season, and waneth and decreaseth another season. And that common English that is spoken in one shire varieth from another. In so much that in my days it happened that certain merchants were in a ship in Thames, for to have sailed over the sea into Zealand, and for lack of wind they tarried at the Foreland, and went to land to refresh themselves. And one of them named Sheffield, a mercer, came to a house and asked for meat; and specially he asked after *eggs*. And the good wife answered that she could speak no French. And the merchant was angry, for he also could speak no French but wanted eggs, and she understood him not. And then, at last, another said he would have *eiren*. Then the good wife said that she understood him well. Lo, what should a man in these days now write, *eggs* or *eiren?* Certainly it is hard to please every man because of diversity and change of language. For in these days, every man that is in any reputation in his district will utter his communication and matters in such manners and terms that few men may understand them. And some honest and great clerks have been with me, and desired me to write the most curious terms that I could find . . . but in my judgment the common terms that daily be used be lighter to be understood than the old and ancient English. . . . Therefore, in a mean between both, I

have reduced and translated this said book into our English, not over rude nor curious, but in such terms as shall be understood, by God's grace. . . .

Caxton's plain style, closer in type to the trade language of London and the East Anglian towns than to official London English or the English of late Middle English literature, is the ancestor of later straightforward communicative writing and of the plain literary style we find in Defoe, Dryden, and many later writers. The homiletical and mystical plain style which attains very great brilliance in that strange, wonderful, and anonymous work *The Cloud of Unknowing,* finally comes into later literature with John Bunyan's *Pilgrim's Progress.*

A.3 During the two centuries after Caxton, the grammar of the standard written language was gradually shaped into something like that of today. The most important development, however, was a process which we may call *Latinization*—the reckless importation of Latin words and grammatical idioms into the language, especially during the flood tide of the Renaissance. If even today a knowledge of Latin is a prerequisite for the etymological understanding of much of our vocabulary, it is due to that development. Thomas Wilson, writing in 1553, thus satirizes the process of Latinization in its worst effects:

> Pondering, *expending* and *revoluting* with my selfe, your *ingent affabilitie,* and *ingenious capacity* for *mundaine* affaires: I cannot but *celebrate,* & *extol* your *magnifical dexteritie* above all other. For how could you have *adepted* such *illustrate* prerogative, and *dominicall superioritie,* if the fecunditie of your *ingenie* had not been so *fertile* and wonderful pregnant. Now therefore being *accersited* to such *splendente* renoume and dignitie splendidious: I doubt not but you will *adjuvate* such poore *adnichilate* orphanes, as whilome war *condisciples* with you, and of *antique*

familiaritie in Lincolnshire. Among whom I being a *scholasticall* panion, *obtestate* your *sublimitie,* to *extoll* mine infirmitie. There is a Sacerdotall dignitie in my *native* Countrey, *contiguate* to me, where I now *contemplate:* which your worshipful benignitie could sone *impetrate* for mee, if it would like you to extend your sedules, and *collaude* me in them to the right honorable lord Chaunceller, or rather Archgrammacian of Englande. You know my literature, you knowe the *pastorall* promotion. I *obtestate* your *clemencie,* to *invigilate* thus much for me, according to my *confidence,* and as you knowe my condigne merites for such a *compendious* living. But now I *relinquish* to *fatigate* your intelligence, with any more *frivolous verbositie,* and therefore he that rules the climates, be evermore your beautreaux, your fortresse, and your bulwarke. Amen.

A.4 The immediate consequence was to pad the vocabulary of written English with elements which, however clear they might be to persons adequately trained in the classics, resisted meaningful analysis by the great bulk of the population. Thus the natural gap between the language of common speech and that of writing was greatly widened. Moreover, at this same time, English acquired the habit, which it still follows, of adapting names for new objects, ideas, and processes from the classical rather than the native word stock. If today the English vocabulary consists of the enormous number of about 700,000 words, most of which are not familiar even to very highly educated persons, it is because of the working out of these tendencies during the succeeding three centuries. Finally, the importation of words through Latinization led directly to the need for books which could explain them. The development of the English dictionary, from Robert Cawdrey's *Table Alphabeticall of Hard Words* (1604), through Johnson's

Dictionary of the English Language (1755), down to our own Webster's, and so forth, was the inevitable result. Today we make increasing use of dictionaries to explain for us much in written English that is unfamiliar.

A.5 By 1700, Renaissance tendencies had become stabilized. A good many Latinisms had been pruned from the language; thousands of others had been absorbed. Under the influence of a tradition of plain writing extending without interruption from Caxton, and seconded by the example of precise French prose, the semi-Latinic syntax of much earlier seventeenth-century writing had given way to a syntax which was more recognizably English. In fact, the rococo world of the late seventeenth and early eighteenth centuries was convinced that written English had finally crystallized into a hard-won perfection comparable with and apparently as unchanging as that of Latin; and it wished to keep it so. From 1664 until the end of the eighteenth century, proposals to establish an English Academy for regulating the language and attempts to establish a definitive dictionary and logical grammar of English were so frequent as to be commonplace. The seeds of linguistic authoritarianism were well sown. None of these things might have come to practical fruition but for the profound sociological and political upheaval known as the Industrial Revolution.

A.6 The fact is, much of the literature of the seventeenth and eighteenth centuries was written for a purely aristocratic audience by literary henchmen sharing the aristocratic predisposition towards unstudied and easy effectiveness. Standardization of spelling and grammar might be advantageous, but it was regarded, very rightly, as the business of the printer and compositor rather than that of the writer. Good writers, even very great writers, often spelled as they felt compelled to spell, and wrote according to a grammar which, since *they* used it, they felt to be completely acceptable. The most cursory glance through a piece of good early eighteenth-century prose will reveal details often ruthlessly condemned in the grammars and dictionaries of then and today: *lie* and *lay* confused; *I sung* as the past tense of *I sing; different than* and *different to* for *different from; between you and I; the largest of the two; this here book* and *that there man; you was* as a plural form, etc. Despite these occurrences, the prose of the early eighteenth century, whether consciously plain, consciously elegant, or consciously rhythmical, is of almost unsurpassed clarity.

A.7 The break in the tradition of written English comes with the Industrial Revolution, which changed the entire class structure of English and, to some extent, of American society. The former aristocracy of landowners gave way politically and socially to a new aristocracy made wealthy by the products of machinery, and drawn, for the most part, from the former mercantile classes. Hitherto, such persons had used written English chiefly as a functional mnemonic device in their business pursuits. Now, suddenly catapulted by wealth into the world of fashion, literature, and literary patronage, they became acutely language conscious. They suddenly realized that linguistic form A was mysteriously less acceptable than linguistic form B, that language, as well as manners, might make the man. Even more than tutoring in deportment, small talk, dancing, and the like, they needed tutoring in language. And they demanded a strict contrast between "white" and "black," an absolute standard of "correctness" to set against absolute "incorrectness," a logical foundation for language which would automatically prescribe the correct form to be used in speech and writing—all this when nothing was really known about the nature of language in general or of the English language in particular.

A.8 Needless to say, by the normal operation of the law of supply and demand, they found precisely what they were seeking. A willing mob of grammarians, pronunciation experts, and dictionary makers rushed to serve them. The first influential grammars, pronunciation treatises, and dictionaries were created to supply their needs. If the serious written English of today is a pruned and regulated language lacking the easy fluency of its seventeenth- and early eighteenth-century ancestor, this is the reason. Correctness became a fetish because it had become a practical social necessity. That fetish, and an entire linguistic philosophy based upon it, has been handed down in lineal succession from the late eighteenth-century grammarians to the author of yesterday's freshman handbook of writing. In 1767, John Buchanan could write as follows without ridicule, for his age knew no better:

> Considering the many grammatical Improprieties to be found in our best Writers, such as Swift, Addison, Pope, etc., a Systematical English syntax is not beneath the Notice of the Learned themselves. Should it be urged, that in the Time of these Writers, English was but a very little subjected to Grammar, that they had scarcely a single Rule to direct them, a question readily occurs. Had they not the Rules of Latin Syntax to direct them?

When we find, as we frequently do, echoes of this statement in grammars written this very year, ridicule seems well justified.

A.9 In this country, the social pressures on the written language were intensified because of the flood of nineteenth-century immigration from Europe. Even to this day, use of the grammar and dictionary and unquestioning belief in the authority of both is far more common in the United States than in Europe. Justifiably so: the primary problem of American education was to